VEGETABLE GROWING
For Health and Flavour

"Courgettes"

Photo: Messrs Sutton & Sons Ltd.

VEGETABLE GROWING
For Health and Flavour

Louis N. Flawn

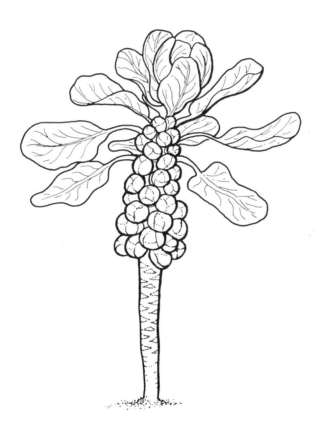

JOHN BARTHOLOMEW AND SON LTD EDINBURGH

First published in Great Britain 1974
by John Bartholomew and Son Ltd,
12 Duncan Street, Edinburgh EH9 1TA and at
216 High Street, Bromley BR1 1PW

ISBN   0 85152   932   1

Printed in Great Britain by
R. & R. Clark Limited, Edinburgh

Contents

Acknowledgements

My sincere thanks are due to those who have helped me with suggestions for this book, and also to those firms who have so kindly allowed the use of their photographs and transparencies.

I am also indebted to my son, V. L. Flawn, N.D.H., for the notes on deep freezing and the chapter on Pests and Diseases and to my erstwhile secretary Mrs F. Chapman who somehow still finds time to cross my T's and who prepared the typescript for this and other books of mine.

L. N. F.

Introduction

Today, the housewife is re-discovering the gastronomical delights of really fresh vegetables and the grower, who for so long has been saturated with the vicarious pleasures of television, is moving his feet from the fireplace to the back garden to do something useful, and in so doing, has that proud sense of achievement that accompanies the proffering of a basket of freshly harvested vegetables to the cook. Philosophy apart, it costs less!

The evidence of the resurgence of interest in vegetable growing lies irrefutably in the rapidly increasing demand for vegetable seeds. This is borne out by leading seedsmen, who report greatly increased sales over the last two years and also by the fuller cultivation of allotments and small gardens.

The escalating cost of vegetables and general living has no doubt prompted many to devote a part of their garden to growing vegetables, thus providing themselves with a healthy hobby and the household with fresh food.

Many people may be starting a garden or allotment for the first time and others already well-versed in other forms of gardening may want to devote just a part of their garden to vegetables. During the last few years many books on gardening subjects have been published but very few on vegetable growing for the beginner. It is hoped that this book will be of help to these beginners and that even the older hand may find in these pages something of interest and help.

The cost of vegetables can be a large proportion of the household budget today and prices continue to rise. In growing your own vegetables you will not only save money but you will be able to enjoy vegetables that are really fresh and to hand when needed. You will be able to enjoy peas and beans picked while they are still young enough to be sweet and tender; potatoes lifted and served while they are unmistakably 'new'— and you can grow the variety you like. There is no need to wait until a crop is heavy; this is often too late to enjoy the real flavour and health-giving properties of young produce. Modern methods and mechanical aids will help you in cultivation and pests can be dealt with, without the risk of poisoning the birds—or yourself.

1 *Making a start*

The would-be gardener is seldom able to choose the site, situation, and soil of his garden. More often the land around the house was chosen simply because it was suitable for building purposes. The purchaser or tenant must take things as he finds them as regards the suitability of the soil for horticultural purposes, and the appearance of the ground around the house may well discourage the most enthusiastic gardener. What was once good arable land may, after some years of neglect, present a depressing picture of thistles, docks, couch-grass and nettles, to say nothing of the builders' rubble. Bad as it may look, it is amazing what can be accomplished in a short time providing the job is tackled in a systematic way, so do not despair.

On the other hand you may be lucky enough to move into a house with a garden that, even though suffering from some neglect, will soon respond to a good clean-up and become productive land. Some improvements and re-planning may be desirable and can be undertaken as time permits.

If the new site is level so much the better, for a sloping garden is much more difficult to cultivate, especially if the slope is steep. Providing it is not too steep it may be possible to form terraces but this involves hard work and the importation of good top-spit soil, but it will greatly ease future cultivation and prevent good soil being gradually washed down towards the bottom of the garden. Very exposed sites can, if the garden is large enough, be given shelter by planting suitable trees or hedges. Damage is often caused in small gardens by cold winds blowing between houses and this should be remedied by means of a hedge or inter-woven fencing panels. In small gardens, hedges that can be kept reasonably dwarf will afford considerable protection for low-growing vegetables.

The amount of preparation and planning neccessary will depend upon whether a completely new site is to be dealt with or whether you happen to be one of the lucky ones to take over a garden which has already been cultivated. In the latter case, straight-forward plain or single-digging, manuring and subsequent breaking down, will render the ground fit for sowing or planting. A good job of single-digging is made by first taking out a trench 15 in. wide and moving the soil near to where digging will finish. Drive the spade down in a vertical position to its full depth and move the soil forward into the trench already taken out, thus leaving another trench. If adding manure it should be spread over the sloping surface of the dug spit so that it becomes well mixed throughout the depth. The process is continued until the end of the plot is reached, where the soil taken out from the first trench will complete the work (*Fig. 1*).

Where the ground around a newly-built house is to be the scene of labour the most important task is to clear the site of builders' rubble. Collect and burn any combustible rubbish and make a heap of any old paint tins and other waste for subsequent carting away or deep burial. Where sub-soil has been left on the surface, which is likely where drains have been laid, then there is little one can do other than distribute the heaps thoroughly. It is likely that you will have to deal with long grass, tall coarse weeds and possibly patches of brambles. Before digging can start these must first be cut down and cleared away. A bagging hook is the best tool for this job providing it is kept sharp, but to the uninitiated it may well

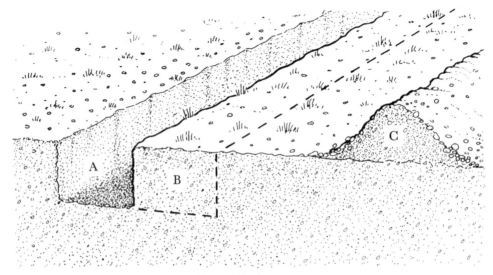

Fig. 1. Single-digging.

A. First trench.
B. Soil from B is turned and moved forward to A.
C. Soil from first trench moved to where digging will finish.

mean a few blisters until the knack of using it is acquired. If you have, or can borrow, a rotary grass cutter it would be an advantage, or alternatively a flame-gun can be used. Advantage should be taken to start a compost heap with any grass and leaves cut down.

Having cleared the ground of long grass and weeds, the next task is to remove any turf. A more satisfactory and long-lasting job is made if the turf is removed rather than attempting to dig it in, as is sometimes advised. A lawn or a weed-free area of grass can be dealt with by chopping the turf into small pieces and burying them in the bottom spit, but if the turf is full of docks, couch grass and other perennial weeds strip off the turves about 1 in. in thickness and 12 in. wide. A turfing iron is the best tool for this job but a sharp spade serves quite well by sliding it under the turf. If the turves are stacked for 12 months they will provide excellent material for putting back into the soil. Stack the turves face downwards dusting the first layer with lime and the next with a sprinkling of sulphate of ammonia. Continue this until the stack is complete.

Now at last the real job of digging can start. Ground that has not been cultivated for some time should be double-dug if good crops are to be the result of these hard

labours. The system of double-digging enables the second spit to be dug or forked through and any 'pan' broken up, thus permitting underlying moisture reserves to be drawn up and deep-rooting subjects to penetrate more easily. It cannot be denied that double-digging is a more laborious job than single-digging but when starting a new site from scratch it is a convenient time to carry out a job that needs doing while the ground is vacant. But do remember never to bring the second spit to the surface.

Begin by digging out a trench across the site 2 ft. wide and 10 or 12 in. deep and barrow the soil to a point near to where digging will finish. Step down into the trench, and, working along, fork through the bottom or second spit. Move the line another 2 ft. and take out the next top spit and place it upside down on the loosened bottom of the first trench. Now get into the new trench and fork it through. Keep a good open trench going with the aid of a line. In this way the top spit is kept on top. It should again be noted that any manure or compost should be scattered evenly over the slope of the top spit. Fork the manure from a conveniently placed heap or two rather than spreading it over the undug ground. This can be a very messy business. Where roots of weeds abound

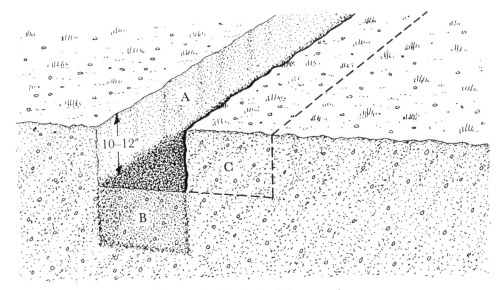

Fig. 2. Double-digging (i), 10–12 in
A. First trench taken out.
B. Second spit of first trench loosened to depth of fork.
C. Top spit of second trench.

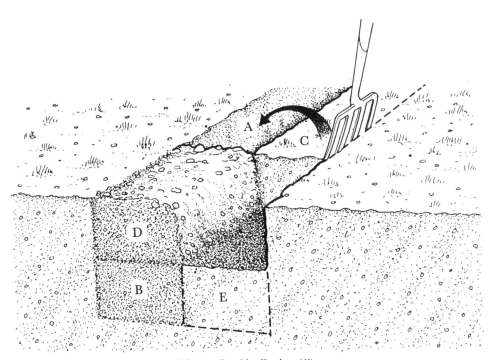

Fig. 3. Double-digging (ii).
A. First trench.
B. Second spit of first trench forked through.
C. Second trench top-soil moved forward to cover B.
D. Soil from C.
E. Bottom of second trench ready to be loosened up.

they must be removed as digging proceeds, taking care to remove every piece that is seen. Have a bucket handy in which to put the weed roots (*Figs. 2 and 3*).

double-digging has been done previously this is deep enough. A larger and more powerful machine will cultivate a wider and deeper strip but a small machine is more

A useful little cultivating machine suitable for the small garden. Many ancillary tools can be fitted. This is the Howard '220'. Photo: Messrs Howard Rotavator Co. Ltd.

The Wolseley Merry Tiller. The new Triton Model with 5 h.p. Briggs and Stratton 4-stroke engine. Will rotavate to a depth of 12 in. Photo: Messrs Wolseley Engineering Ltd.

Digging can be a back-aching job when one is not used to it so take it steady. Dig to the full depth of the spade but take out a width of spit you can comfortably lift and turn over rather than trying to rush the work by taking out heavier spits than you can easily manage. Work steadily, for there is no point in overdoing it and spending the next two or three days in bed.

Subsequent cultivation can be done with one of the small machines now available. Properly used these little machines do an excellent job and save no end of time and hard work. There is a large range of these machines to choose from. Their prices vary in accordance with their design and power and it is possible to hire a machine from some gardening shops and garden centres. These light machines will cultivate to a depth of 6 in. on most soils, and where

conveniently used on a small area and in a confined space.

It might be advisable to say a word here regarding tools. It is really surprising how few are needed at the outset and equally surprising how many one can find oneself with after a few years.

A cheap spade is a false economy, so get the best you can afford—a stainless one if funds will run to it. An old and badly worn spade with rounded corners and half the blade worn away will never do a good job of digging; neither will a rusty or dirty one. A four-pronged digging fork is required for use when ground needs shaking up to remove weeds or for surface treatment. A swan-neck draw hoe is essential for earthing up, taking out wide drills or when dealing with weeds and general hoeing. A 6-in. and a 4-in. are useful sizes. There is also the push

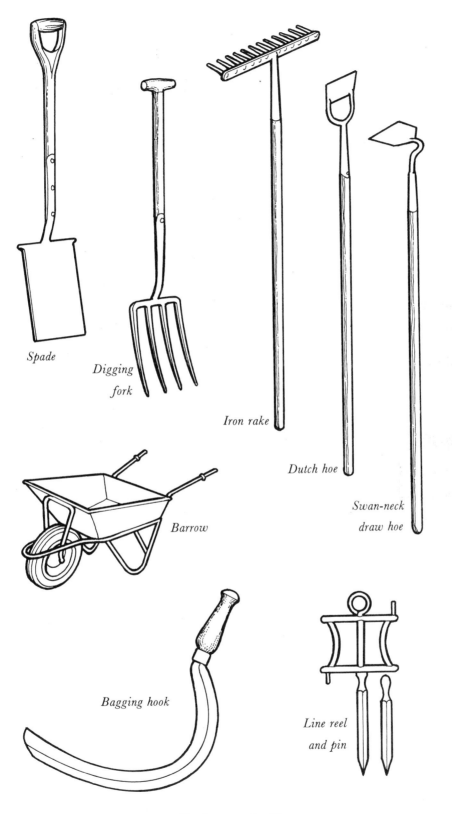

Spade

Digging
fork

Iron rake

Dutch hoe

Swan-neck
draw hoe

Barrow

Bagging hook

Line reel
and pin

Tools to start with

or Dutch hoe. This has the advantage over the draw hoe that it is easy to use and as one walks backward while hoeing the freshly moved soil is not trodden on. A wheel hoe can be a time-saving tool on a large plot. A light wheelbarrow will save a lot of time and energy.

The rake is necessary to finally clear off larger portions of soil and any rubbish and to bring the surface to a fine and level tilth ready for sowing. An iron rake is used for this purpose. A good strong garden line is needed and this is best wound on to a reel and the other end tied to an iron pin. Such a line will remain taut. A trowel and a dibber will be needed for planting out, and where patches of bramble or long grass are to be dealt with, a bagging or swop hook will be required.

Such a collection of tools will be adequate for a start and you can add to them as the occasion arises. If you keep them clean and free from rust they will last for many years. Clean tools not only last better when looked after but they make the job so much easier. It is astonishing how much easier it is to work with a well polished spade, and my advice is to get into the habit of cleaning the tools after using them. Now and again give the cleaned tools a wipe over with an oily rag. Old sump oil does nicely.

2 The Soil and planning

After a spell of digging it will not come amiss to relax in a comfortable armchair with a glass of whatever the favourite tipple may be and give some thought to the soil you have been bending your back over. As gardeners we should know something of the soil we are to work, if our efforts are to be worthwhile. It is impossible in a book of this kind to go into details of origin and structure, neither is it necessary. The reader who may be interested in the geology of our soils should consult a book on that subject.

Soils vary greatly and we must accept them as we find them, working each to the best advantage and improving the less kindly types as far as possible by suitable cultivation. We may have a clay soil that, because of its heaviness, is difficult to cultivate or a light loam with perfect drainage that will be easier to work and produce a very high quality of vegetables with far less trouble. A light sandy soil will be the easiest to work but sadly deficient in humus, hungry and liable to dry out very quickly.

Soil has originated from rocks which through the course of millions of years have been broken down into tiny particles. Animal and plant life have combined in this process to form what we know as soil. The tiny particles have often been washed down by rivers and inundations or blown long distances by winds.

Generally speaking five main types of soil will be met with: clay, loam, chalk, sand and peat.

A clay soil. Clay soil consists of very tiny particles that adhere so closely together that a sample resembles putty. It is heavy and very retentive of moisture and impossible to work in wet weather. A garden with such a soil should be dug in the autumn and the surface left rough so that as much as possible is left exposed to the weather. Frosts and winds will do a great deal towards breaking it down so that in the spring it will be easier to reduce to the tilth needed for sowing and planting. Spring sowings will be later than on the lighter lands but clay has the advantage that it does not dry out so quickly in the summer. It is, however, liable to crack badly and the hoe should be kept working to prevent large fissures appearing.

Clay soils need regular liming. This will help to prevent the particles clinging together and render the soil less sticky and binding. The addition of grit, sharp sand, bonfire ash, strawy manure and composted straw will all help to make it more workable. Clay soils are usually low in nitrogen and this should be corrected. Good drainage is essential and if there is a convenient ditch it pays to drain the land well. This is difficult where no ditch or stream is available and the only alternative is to dig a really large soakaway and drain into this. A clay soil is difficult soil to work but once broken down and tamed it will produce wonderful crops.

A loamy soil. The ideal soil is a light loam of good depth, dark and overlying a somewhat heavier sub-soil that is well drained. The gardener with such a soil can count himself lucky for it will be kindly, mellow, warm and capable of producing first-class crops. Loam is a mixture of clay and sand. What is known as a sandy or light loam will contain a high proportion of sand while a heavy loam will consist of more clay than sand. Both will have a high humus content.

Loams do not dry out quickly nor do they 'pan' down hard as will clay. Loams are very workable and the gardener with a good loamy soil will have the best of all soils.

A sandy soil. Here we have the exact opposite to a clay soil. It is very easily worked at all times of the year and it is usually well drained and warms up quickly in the spring. Being coarse-grained it does not retain moisture and therefore dries out quickly. It is very deficient of humus and demands constant replacement of organic matter. It is also deficient of potash. Pig and cow manure with plenty of straw or well-made compost make excellent organic replacements.

A sandy soil may well be known as a hungry soil for it has little retentive power for plant nutrients. It is an advantage to be able to work on the land a few hours after a heavy downpour of rain and with liberal manuring it can be very productive, especially for early cropping.

A chalky soil. This is one of the most difficult types of soil to manage. It lacks both humus and plant foods. Double-digging is called for more regularly than with some other soils because under the top few inches a sheer bed of chalk may exist. This must be broken up and organic matter should be mixed in with the second spit as well as the top. Do not, if you are cultivating on chalk, remove all the stones, as they help to conserve moisture and keep the soil cool in the summer. Avoid walking or working on chalk during wet weather. Like clay it is a soil that takes time to tame but once in trim it can be very productive. I remember seeing on an allotment site near Croydon some of the finest crops of onions and greenstuff I have ever seen on any allotment—and on a very chalky site.

A peaty soil. Here is another difficult soil to manage. It will consist almost entirely of organic matter—the residue of decayed water and bog plants. Such soils are often badly drained. Heavy dressings of lime are needed to counteract the acidity produced by the decaying matter. Annual dressings of lime up to 8 oz. per square yard may be necessary. Phosphates and potash will also be needed. Fortunately peat soils are easy to work but the question of drainage should be examined. Hard work and perseverance will work wonders as may be seen in the gardens of some of the moorland cottages.

The sub-soil. Top-soils will vary in depth from a few inches to some 18 in. or more, an average depth being about 12 in. The sub-soil is that part of the soil lying immediately below this and may be similar in type to the top-soil or entirely different. It is often hard and infertile and should not be brought to the surface when double-digging. Some sub-soils, such as clay, will more often than not be poorly-drained and liable to flooding or water-logging unless drainage is created. A light soil overlying a sub-soil such as sand or gravel will be liable to dry out very quickly and organic matter should be incorporated with the second spit when digging. A hard red sandy layer just below the top spit will sometimes be found and this must be broken up using a pick-axe or a mattock. On hillsides there may only be a few inches of soil over hard rock and very little can be done except to add as much in the way of soil and humus-making material as can be obtained.

Planning. The average allotment is only 10 rods in area and the small garden is usually no bigger. Some gardens will be long and narrow, others broad and short with a variety of soils and vastly differing climatic conditions, and it is impossible to suggest a lay-out that will meet any general plan. There are, however, a number of points that should be considered before laying out a new garden and these should be studied before starting, otherwise a great deal of time and effort may be wasted by essential alterations later on. Too much planning will be tedious to the busy man but a little forethought and a rough sketch could save time and trouble later.

Only you know how you want to lay out your garden. You will no doubt want a lawn, if only for the wife to push the pram on to, and perhaps room for a shady seat where you can relax after a spell on the vegetable plot. A flower border surrounding the lawn certainly adds colour and lends interest.

The lawn should be sited near to the house and where possible be screened from the vegetable plot, which is usually positioned farthest from the house. The prospect from the dining-room window is more pleasing if it overlooks a neatly trimmed lawn and attractive borders rather than rows of cabbages.

The rows in the vegetable garden should run as near as possible from north to south, thus ensuring a good share of the sun on either side of the rows, but don't worry if your rows must go east to west. In a small garden the short rows permit a greater variety than with long rows where the number will be limited. It makes things messy and more complicated if several kinds of vegetables need to be grown in one long row.

A south border will be the warmest and earliest site in the garden although to take advantage of such a border the rows may have to be short. Such a border backed by a wall or fence will make a suitable place for the first early carrots, peas, lettuce etc. A similar border facing west will be useful for early sowing and more particularly for seed beds. The north border and the east will be shady and at times exposed, but useful for late cropping.

Do not be tempted to make a maze of paths in a vegetable garden since they rob you of valuable space in just the same way as motor roads take up so much valuable farming land. Paths are necessary it is true but one good hard path will normally serve. Other paths that may be necessary at certain times can be temporary, and narrow and simply trodden firm, to be dug over as soon as the need for them ceases.

The main path should be a good one and regardless of the surface material a good foundation should be laid. Take off any turf and excavate to a depth of a few inches. Fill in with breeze, broken bricks and gravel, and make this firm using a heavy bolster. You need a thickness of 2 in. of concrete over the breeze or bricks. Boards of 2 to 3 in. in width should be pegged firmly along each side, taking care to get the levels right and the boards parallel. This edging will contain the cement until it has set. Provided you have pegged the boards level the wet concrete can be finished off to a nice flat surface with a heavy piece of wood by laying it across the side pieces and zigzagging it along. Do not try to smooth off the surface but leave it slightly rough because a path smoothed off with a trowel or float could be a source of danger in frosty weather. A well-made path will last for many years and help to lighten your labours. A quicker job can be made by excavating as described and filling up with gravel, which must be well rolled down. The surface can be treated with one of the bituminous preparations made for this purpose.

In making your plan don't forget that you will need room for a garden frame. This should be situated on a south or south-west border. Also remember that you will need a shady place for the compost heap.

Cropping and Rotation. Much has been written on cropping and elaborate plans drawn up showing how an allotment or a small garden can be cropped to the best advantage but no standard plan has yet been made to suit the individual case. We do need to make the most of a small garden but we also want to grow those crops we like and which suit our purpose best. If we grow something we do not want for the sake of maintaining a certain rotation we waste both time and land and could find ourselves with a crop of unwanted cabbages whereas peas and beans might have been more useful.

So what to grow? Once the soil has been prepared it will grow any kind of vegetable. Yours is the choice, and you can select your favourite vegetables bearing in mind that perishable produce such as peas, beans, lettuce etc. gathered fresh from one's own garden are tastier than those which have been harvested a day or two before and which have travelled long distances to market, and then to the shop, and been displayed. But stored vegetables, i.e. beetroot, parsnips, potatoes and root vegetables generally, do not differ a great deal whether you take them from your own clamp or from the shop. But in their early stages of growth beetroot, carrots, turnips and new potatoes can be a very different matter. These are at their best when young and quite small but particularly at this time they are expensive to buy and it is well worth while to find room for the early roots and miss out the later types.

And so with potatoes. We all, I think, look forward to new potatoes and enjoy the maincrop varieties but once again our limited space may mean that we can only find room for a few rows of earlies and no room for the late types.

When we speak of a rotation we have in mind a system whereby a crop of the same class or with similar characteristics does not follow another of the same class or group. If a crop of one class is grown on the same site continuously it exhausts the available supplies of food in the soil and the crop ceases to be profitable. There is also the possibility of disease being carried over from one year to the next. The soil requirements of various crops differ to some extent. Parsnips and carrots need a deeper soil than, say, cabbage and their long roots tap and release plant nutrients that would otherwise be locked up. Some crops need more lime than others (brassicas) while another (potatoes) does not need so much. Peas and beans like a soil rich in manure. Roots do not require fresh manure. A proper rotation takes these varying needs into account and by changing the position of crops each year and liming or manuring as required the crops can be given the conditions they need.

Crop rotation is a simple matter in ordinary farming or in a very large garden but becomes a very different matter when applied to the small plot, since the garden must be divided into three or four more or less equal plots each planted with a different group of crops. This becomes impossible to carry out satisfactorily in a small garden as the crops to be grown are those that the household has most need of and it is possible that no potatoes at all, or very few, will be

	1st year	2nd year	3rd year
Plot 1	Potatoes	Roots	Brassicas
Plot 2	Roots	Brassicas	Potatoes
Plot 3	Brassicas	Potatoes	Roots

Fig. 4. A three-course rotation. Not an ideal rotation but provides for deep and shallow cultivation, manuring and a change of site. Peas, beans, onions, leeks etc. can be grown at either end of plots 1 or 3. Plot 1 (1st year) should be turned and manured but no lime given. Plot 2 should not be manured. Plot 3 will need manuring when digging is done and lime applied to the surface later.

grown and only a few if any of rootcrops. The main interest will be in salads, peas, beans, spinach, a few greens and perhaps one or two permanent crops.

But although on the small plot a true rotation will be difficult to follow an effort must be made to change the crops over to another site each year. Where space permits and a larger variety of vegetables can be grown a proper rotation can be followed with perhaps some slight modification.

The diagram (*Fig. 4*) shows a simple three-course rotation. Here the garden is divided into three plots and vegetables bracketed into three main groups and grown on different plots each year: (1) the cabbage family (this will include turnips); (2) root crops; (3) potatoes. Peas, beans, onions and leeks will be planted at either end of Plots 1 and 3. Both onions and runner beans are frequently grown on the same site each year but must be given a fresh site if the yield falls off through disease. In this way the plants can be given the conditions and treatment they prefer and the plan should be followed as closely as possible. A four-course rotation is even better but needs four plots (*Fig. 5*).

	1st year	2nd year	3rd year	4th year
Plot 1	Potatoes	Peas & Beans	Brassicas	Roots
Plot 2	Peas & Beans	Brassicas	Roots	Potatoes
Plot 3	Brassicas	Roots	Potatoes	Peas & Beans
Plot 4	Roots	Potatoes	Peas & Beans	Brassicas

Fig. 5. A four-course rotation. Plot 3 (1st year) can include onions, leeks, celery etc. Where only a few potatoes are needed they can be grown on plot 1.

3 Food for plants

We have seen how soils vary both in structure and degree of fertility. Soils that at some time have been cultivated will be reasonably fertile for the soil will contain a certain amount of humus and although fertility may have dropped it can be improved and maintained by regular dressings of organic manures, bag fertilizers and lime.

There are some types of soil that are 'raw' and which consist almost entirely of clay, chalk, sand etc. It is not often that these are encountered unless the garden happens to be on a site that was once a sand or gravel pit or on a moor. Such soils however, can be made to produce healthy crops by first improving the physical condition, by draining and incorporating suitable material to improve the texture, and then building up fertility by working in humus-forming material and fertilizers.

Humus. This is vitally necessary in building up and maintaining fertility. It is the organic material found in the soil and is formed from the decaying parts of plants and animals and the residue of previous dressings of manure or compost. It is dark brown or nearly black in colour and therefore tends to make the soil warmer and, like a sponge, it readily takes up moisture and holds it in reserve. A soil rich in humus may be said to be warmer and more retentive of moisture.

Never think of the soil as just 'dirt'. It is by no means an inert mass. If it were, nothing would grow in it. It is in a sense a factory in which countless millions of workers are constantly carrying on a business that brings about fertility and on which our existence depends. Bacteria of many kinds, moulds, yeasts, fungi and many burrowing creatures all play a part in breaking down to a simple chemical, the food which plants must have.

The presence of organic material such as animal manure and decaying vegetation, is essential if this unseen population is to be maintained, and unless humus-forming material is dug in from time to time, their numbers will diminish and fertility will be lowered.

Humus is found in the top 10 in. or so where the soil is warmer and it is here that the bacteria and other organisms are mostly found. For this reason the top spit should not be buried when digging.

Plant foods or nutrients fall into three classes:

1. *Nitrates* which supply nitrogen.
2. *Phosphates* which supply phosphoric acid.
3. *Potassium* salts which supply potash.

Carbon dioxide is also needed but this is obtained by the leaves from the air.

Nitrogen encourages growth of leaf and stem and is specially needed for vegetables grown for their leaves, e.g. cabbage, lettuce, spinach etc. Nitrogen is quickly washed out of the soil.

Phosphatic acid promotes root growth and seed formation and helps toward early production.

Potash checks unrestricted growth and helps to ensure healthy plants.

Organic manures

Stable manure is the dung and litter from horses. It should contain plenty of litter in the shape of straw, bracken or peat, which will be saturated with urine from the horses. It is a 'hot' manure and ferments quickly and is very suitable for making a hotbed. It is the best kind of manure to buy if you can get it. Horse manure is best for the heavier soils.

Farmyard manure. This is mostly made up of cow and pig manure with sometimes a little horse manure mixed in. It is important that it should contain plenty of litter but a sample that contains a lot of wood chippings or sawdust should be avoided.

Cow manure. This is a cold manure and very loose. It is best used on light land and needs plenty of litter. This should be straw. It is improved by stacking and additional straw can be added when doing this. It decomposes slowly and is more suitable for light soils.

Pig manure. This is another 'cold' and loose manure and probably the best for a sandy soil so long as it contains plenty of litter. This again is better if it can be stacked for a time.

Poultry manure. Poultry manure is best used as a side-dressing after drying and powdering. It is an unbalanced manure with a high nitrogen content but very little phosphates and only a very small potash content.

The balance of nitrogen, phosphates and potash in these organic manures varies a great deal according to the way the animals are fed and bedded and the way it is stacked. The value of such material lies in the fact that it contains so much bulky vegetable remains in the shape of urine-soaked litter so that besides supplying nitrogen, phosphates and potash a liberal amount of humus-forming material is made available.

An average dressing of such manure would be about one good barrow-load to 10 square yards.

Substitute for manures

Unfortunately manure is hard to come by in these days of the internal combustion engine and we must often look elsewhere for organic replacements. This is so important that a short section will be found on page 29.

Green manuring is a way of adding organic matter to the soil and a part of the garden that is going to be vacant for a time can be sown with lupins, clover, rape or rye and dug in as green manure to decay. Rye is a favourite plant for this purpose and can be sown in the summer or early autumn and dug in during the next February. Do not sow rape or mustard on land where there is club root. The quantity of rye to sow would be roughly 3 oz. to a rod of ground.

Spent hops. This forms an excellent substitute for manure but you need a dressing of fertilizer as well. A nearby brewery might supply, or spent hops can sometimes be had through the trading store of an allotment society.

Seaweed. Unfortunately this is only available if you live by the seaside. The best types to use are kelp (*Laminaria*) or bladder wrack (*Fulvus*). These seaweeds are almost as valuable as farmyard manure but are low in phosphates. They should be applied in the autumn or winter.

Shoddy. Wool shoddy from a factory is obtainable in industrial centres. It is more easily obtainable in the more northern districts and although low in nitrogen it makes excellent humus replacements.

Sewage sludge. This is little used in private gardens but makes a good humus replacement and is looked on as more of a soil improver than a manure.

Peat. There are two kinds of peat that will interest the vegetable grower—sedge peat and moss peat. Sedge peat is on the whole the best as it will be broken down more quickly than moss peat. But moss or sphagnum peat will be better for the gardener who wants to increase the moisture-holding capacity of a light land. The use of peat as a soil conditioner is too well-known to dwell on here and it is very useful as a mulch. It is free from weeds and disease spore but has no manural value.

Peat should be moistened before applying to the land. It is rather difficult to thoroughly dampen but if you are dealing with a bale break it up into a flattened heap and pour water on it. It does not easily soak up the water and the only way to wet it is to keep turning over the heap as the water is applied and to trample on it and press it well down and keep repeating the process until the whole is wet right through. This can be a long job. Water is better applied via a fine rose.

Inorganic fertilizers

Inorganic fertilizers are a supplement to, and not substitutes for, organic manures.

These fertilizers will only replace exhausted food supplies but organic manures will replace both food and humus. Those that supply nitrogen are:

Nitrate of soda. This is a quick-acting fertilizer that can be used as a side-dressing in the spring.

Sulphate of ammonia. Slower in action than the above and is used with other fertilizers to make up a complete dressing. Also used as a side-dressing.

Hoof and horn. Hoof and horn meal breaks down slowly, releasing its nitrogen over a long period. It is used in complete dressings and is an organic substance.

Nitro chalk. Another fertilizer that can be used as a side-dressing as it acts fairly quickly. It has a more sustained effect than nitrate of soda and can be used on more advanced plants.

Those that supply phosphoric acid are:

Superphosphate of lime. Usually used with other fertilizers to make a complete dressing.

Basic slag. A by-product from steel works. It should be applied in the autumn and spread for a period before digging in. It contains some lime.

Bone meal. The residue left after fats and gelatine have been removed. It is slow in action. Bone flour is ground more finely and is rather quicker in action. Bone meal is, like hoof and horn, organic but it is convenient to mention it here. It is used as part of a complete dressing.

Those that supply potash:

Sulphate of potash. Probably the best fertilizer to use in the potash group and used largely in complete fertilizers. It is also used as a side-dressing when a known shortage of potash exists. A dressing in this case of 1 oz. per square yard is given.

Muriate of potash. This is a more impure product than sulphate of potash and not generally recommended for vegetable crops.

Kainit. This is a natural potash salt from mines in Germany. It should be applied in the autumn when the ground is fallow.

Nitrate of potash and *phosphate of potash.* These are both excellent fertilizers that supply in the former case nitrogen as well as potash and in the latter phosphates as well as potash. They are expensive fertilizers and are used in the greenhouse rather than in the open.

A complete fertilizer has been mentioned several times in this section, and refers to a balanced ration suitable for general purposes. There are many formulae but if you want to make your own the salts can all be obtained at any garden shop. Here is the formula:

Sulphate of ammonia   7 parts ⎫
Superphosphate of lime 14 parts ⎬ by
Bone flour   7 parts ⎪ weight
Sulphate of potash   7 parts ⎭

The ingredients must be crushed and well mixed and applied at the rate of 3 oz. per square yard.

Proprietary mixtures can be purchased ready to use and these are quite satisfactory, providing they are used in accordance with the makers' directions.

Do not be tempted to use fertilizer in any haphazard way; you will probably do more harm than good and finish up with a very unbalanced soil. If your cultivation at the outset is sound you won't need to play with chemicals during the growing season.

Lime

The presence of lime in the soil is highly important and especially so where vegetables are concerned, and it is only where lime is present that bag fertilizers can be used to the full advantage. Lime counteracts the acidity produced in the process of decay and will also free locked up reserves of phosphate and potash. It is needed to some extent as a plant food. An excess of lime will cause trouble by inducing deficiencies in certain trace elements such as manganese and iron. Some soils have reserves of lime that will last for many years, while others are deficient. The dangers of too much lime are, however, far less than the danger from under-liming.

It is an advantage to have the soil tested, especially when starting a new garden. A rough and ready test is to take samples of soil over the area to a depth of 3 or 4 in. and mix them together. From the whole take a small sample and place in a tumbler adding just enough water to make a thick paste. Into this pour a little hydrochloric acid diluted to twice its volume with water. A great deal of effervescence will indicate that lime is present in fair quantity but if few bubbles appear lime will be badly needed.

Although a satisfactory basic guide, this test gives no real idea as to how much lime is needed and a better method is to use a B.D.H. Soil Indicator. An indicating fluid added to the sample of soil will give a colour reaction varying from blue to red and this can be matched against a colour chart which gives a more accurate guide to the amount of lime needed. You can get a soil test made that will show the real state of your soil as regards availability of lime and plant nutrients. This will be done free for you by your County Horticultural Dept. and you can then apply the correct amount of fertilizers and lime to ensure a correct balance.

In the garden, hydrated lime is the most convenient form of lime to use. It has been slaked in the process of manufacture, and is purchased as a fine powder which is dry and non-caustic. It can be applied at all seasons. A normal dressing would be 7 oz. to each square yard and should be distributed over the surface of the soil.

Lime should always be used for brassicas, peas and beans but it is not so essential for potatoes and roots. A dressing of 7 oz. per square yard each year on the site where the cabbages are to be grown will keep the soil in good condition.

There are other forms of lime, for example quicklime and carbonate of lime, but these are more difficult to handle and far less convenient for use in the average small garden, than hydrated lime.

4 Cultivation, sowing and planting

The successful culture of vegetables rests to a large extent on the careful initial cultivation of the ground and, except for the special attention which each kind needs, subsequent care is a matter of applying a few rules and using one's common sense.

The beginner is sometimes puzzled as to when to sow. This of course depends on when you want to harvest the crop but most of us like to be able to enjoy our crops as early as possible, which means early sowing. Even so it is no use sowing until the soil is in a condition to work on and for this we are at the mercy of the weather, and must wait until the soil is warmer and drier. More harm than good is done by working on the soil too soon. A good test is if the soil still sticks to your boots, then it is too soon to start work on it.

We are sometimes advised to sow seeds on a certain date but our fickle climate does not permit any hard and fast rules and we must just use our own common sense and get down to sowing when climatic and soil conditions are favourable, even if our sowings have to be delayed for a month. It is a fact that in a late season long periods of good growing weather often follow on from bad weather, and the harvest is good and plentiful, in spite of late sowings. We must also remember that in some parts of the country we are faced with longer and more severe winters and shorter summers. Sowing dates in those regions will be later than in the more favoured districts.

The seed bed. If the soil has been dug in the autumn and left rough for the weather to break down the first job in the early days is to fork it through, breaking up any remaining lumps into smaller pieces. At this time any fertilizers needed can be added, or lime spread over the newly forked ground. On lighter soils where digging has been deferred this should now be done. In either case the work should be carried out some time in advance of sowing.

A few fine days in spring will render the soil workable and it should then be forked through again but only lightly—a depth of two or three inches only. Light soils will present no difficulty; it is the heavier soils that bother one for they may reach just the right degree of dryness when the amateur gardener is otherwise engaged. For if we must wait until the weekend, and then it rains, the soil becomes too wet again and sowing must be delayed. The gardener must be ready to seize the opportunity as it is offered on those heavier soils. Neither must he wait until an April sun has baked the clods hard. A useful tool in dealing with such soil is the Canterbury hoe. It has three long and rather broad sharpened tines which will cut into the clods, or a hard blow with the back of the hoe will break them up. Other soils can be reduced by shallow forking over and breaking any larger pieces by hitting them sideways with the back of the fork held almost flat.

Some firming will be necessary and on a not too heavy soil this can be done by treading over the area with a shuffling motion. But do not overdo it; the pressure given must be governed by the amount of moisture in the soil.

Raking down. This can now be done. For this you will need an iron rake and a fairly wide one. First lightly rake off the larger stones and any rubbish and then rake the surface to a fine tilth and leave it level. Bend your back well down so that the handle of the rake is not at too steep an angle and do not press deeply into the soil for it is only the top inch that needs to be dealt with. Use short strokes. A large wooden rake is often used on a heavier soil for the initial raking.

Drawing the drills. Next the drills must be drawn out. You will need a strong garden line which should be drawn taut so that the drill is really straight. The best tool for taking out a drill is the corner of a swan-necked hoe. Draw in short strokes against the line making sure it does not bow by lightly placing one foot on the line as you work backwards. Keep the drill at an even depth otherwise germination will be irregular. Some like to use a stick for shallow drills.

Wide, flat-bottomed drills are made for peas and beans instead of the usual V-shaped drill. These can be made with a broad hoe. One sometimes reads 'take out a wide drill 3 in. deep'. This is not so easy on a heavy soil and you may find it much easier to use a spade for the job. A narrow border spade is just the tool.

How deep should drills be? Here the commonsense part of gardening comes in again. Instructions on seed packets and in books must be regarded as an indication. The type of soil must be considered, for on a light soil that dries out very quickly the drills can be a little deeper. An average depth would be $\frac{3}{4}$ to 1 in. for the larger seeds such as beetroot, parsnips, etc. while smaller seeds such as radish, cabbage, etc. would need a depth of $\frac{1}{2}$ in. The smallest seeds such as cauliflower would need only a light covering and the seedbed should of course be well cultivated. The really large seeds of peas can go $2\frac{1}{2}$ in. deep and beans at 3 in.

Sowing the seed. It is more customary to sow continuously along the drill but some prefer to sow at spaced intervals. In the case of lettuce for example we know that the plants will need thinning to stand at 10 in. apart. There is a considerable saving in seed and later in time spent on thinning out if only 4 or 5 seeds are dropped at intervals of 10 ins. Now that pelleted seed is readily obtainable it is very easy to do this. Some seeds are better sown in a continuous row: carrots and onions for example. If sown thinly enough, very little thinning will be needed later and most of the thinnings will be just big enough to eat. In the case of salad onions no thinning will be necessary.

The great thing to learn in sowing is to sow thinly. Several methods can be adopted. A little seed can be tipped into one hand and with the fingers of the other hand drop it into the drill. The practised sower will put some seed into one hand and closing the fingers trickle the seed past the first finger and thumb, holding the hand fingers upwards over the drill (*Fig. 6*). This needs a bit of practice as the seed is apt to get between

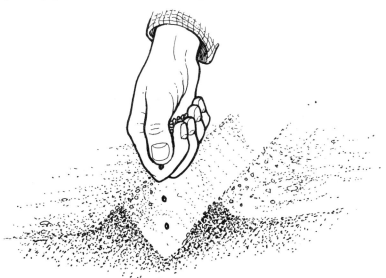

Fig. 6. Sowing the seed.

the fingers and in getting it back into the palm it is spilled and you find later on you have sown lettuce or some other vegetable all over the place. It is a help to mix small seeds with some sand. Another method is to use a nail to make a hole a little bigger than the seed, in the bottom of a cocoa or similar tin. Put a little seed in the tin and using it like a pepper pot shake the seed along the drill. Be sure to pierce the hole through the bottom from the inside, otherwise the seed will not trickle out. This sounds like a very amateurish way, but it works. Always keep the hand well down over the drill, especially when there is a wind blowing. The larger seeds present no difficulty and the really big ones like peas and beans should always be sown singly.

On lighter soils the seed can be covered in by shuffling the feet along either side of the drill and pushing in the soil. Otherwise cover up by carefully pulling the soil over with the rake, not forgetting to mark and label the ends of the row. Now work along the drill and lightly tamp the soil down over the drill with the rake (*Fig. 7*). Remove the line and rake off level.

Where birds are a nuisance it is as well to give some protection by placing netting or pea guards over the rows. Twiggy sticks layed on the ground will help and these will keep off the cats as well as the birds.

When the seedlings are really growing well see that they do not crowd each other out. They must have room to develop and early thinning is very necessary. Thin out during showery weather but when the foliage is dry, and make the soil firm round any seedlings that may have been loosened. Do not attempt to thin to the final distance at one go. When the seed has been sown at intervals some thinning will be needed and it is better to thin down to three and later to leave the most promising seedling to mature.

Transplanting. Very few vegetables other than brassicas are transplanted, apart from tomatoes, marrows etc., which will be dealt with later. The brassicas are sometimes pricked out from the seed bed to a nursery bed. This encourages a nice fibrous root system and a short-jointed plant. From the nursery bed they are moved to their permanent quarters. Leeks and autumn-sown onions are moved from the seed bed to where they are to mature.

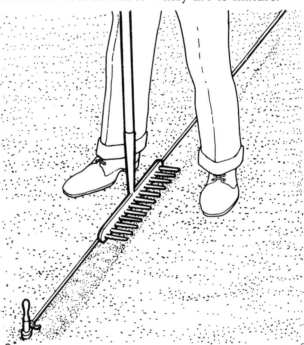

Fig. 7. Tamping down after sowing to ensure good contact with seed and soil.

Before transplanting or pricking out, the seed or nursery bed should be well watered some hours previously. Needless to say the ground in which the plants are to go must also be moist. Dull and showery weather is, of course, the ideal time to do this.

Either a dibber or a trowel can be used when planting out brassicas. The dibber is a favourite tool and more generally used. In planting out be sure that the dibber hole is deep enough (but not too deep) to allow the roots to hang down without being doubled up. In using the dibber make the hole and lower the plant so that the bottom leaves are almost touching the soil. Holding the plant, thrust the dibber into the soil a few inches to one side of the plant and lever it over towards the plant thus closing up the first hole and firming the plant. There is no need to keep jabbing at the soil round the stem to firm

the plant. You will probably injure the stem in doing so. (*Fig. 8*).

A better job of planting is accomplished with a trowel, although the work is not done so quickly. Cauliflowers to my mind should always be planted with a trowel so that the right depth of planting can be assured and the roots given a better spread than when confined to a dibber hole. Apart from its use when planting brassicas, leeks and onions, the dibber can be a dangerous tool and even with the plants mentioned damage is often caused by careless handing.

Hoeing. The hoe is a most valuable garden tool and its use assists in keeping down unwanted weeds as well as in earthing-up and drawing drills. The use of the hoe will ensure a loose mulch on the surface and prevent panning after heavy or constant rain. The Dutch hoe is particularly useful.

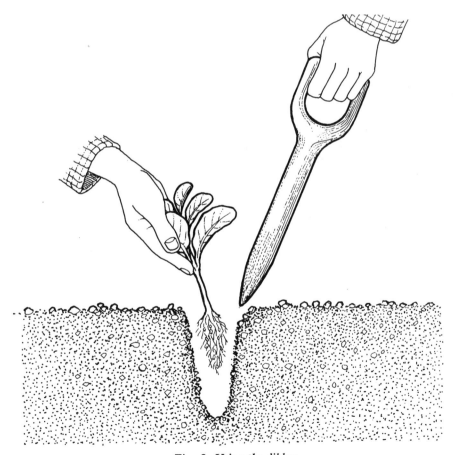

Fig. 8. Using the dibber.

It is also known as the push hoe because it is pushed by the operator, who walks backwards and not over the freshly hoed soil. It is quick and easy to use. The draw hoe is different in that it is drawn towards the cultivator who must walk forward over the soil already hoed. The hoe should be constantly used on the heavier soils, which are liable to develop cracks during very dry weather. Constant hoeing will do much to prevent these cracks becoming quite large fissures and thus help to conserve moisture.

Considerable attention over the last three or four years has been drawn to a method of controlling weeds between growing plants by means of paraquat and diquat. These chemicals are applied in solution over the weeds by means of a special spray bar fitted to a watering can that enables the weeds to be dealt with close up to the plants. The spray becomes inactive on reaching the soil but care must be taken not to allow it to touch the foliage of the plants. This method permits weeds to be destroyed without disturbing the soil and bringing fresh seeds to the surface to germinate.

Paraquat and diquat can be had under the proprietory name of 'Weedol' from garden shops and garden centres together with a special applicator for applying the spray. Both of these are poisonous and like all garden weedkillers and fertilizers should be kept in their correct containers, clearly labelled and stored out of reach of children. *Note.* Paraquat and diquat are supplied in wettable powder form in packets.

Using the Dutch hoe. A most useful tool for keeping down weed growth and maintaining a surface tilth.

Treating weeds with 'Weedol', which now contains diquat and paraquat. Inter-row weeding is achieved by fitting a shorter spray bar to the applicator or can. Photo: Messrs Imperial Chemical Industries Ltd.

5 *The compost heap*

It has already been emphasized that the replacement of organic matter in the soil is essential. At one time the easy way to do this was to order a load of manure and dig this in. This is seldom possible now and almost impossible for the town dweller. The shortage of natural manure has led to the conversion of vegetable waste from the garden into manure. Well-made compost will be equal to farmyard manure, sometimes better, and often contains as much nitrogen, phosphates and potash.

The basic principle in making compost is that when vegetable matter, soil, water and air are brought together plus nitrogen, fermentation is brought about and this converts the material into humus. A small amount of lime is also needed to counteract the acidity brought about by the breaking-down process. The heap must therefore be made in such a way that these conditions can be produced and the right type of bacteria encouraged. Any haphazard method must be avoided since a mere heap of old leaves and weeds carelessly thrown into a corner will not serve any good purpose.

Always build the heap directly on the soil and not on boards or a concrete floor. Start by putting down a layer of coarse material to permit air to circulate from the bottom. Next place a 6- to 8-in. layer of vegetable waste. This should be a mixture of soft and harder material such as cabbage leaves, weeds, grass cuttings etc. mixed with soft hedge trimmings, cut up cabbage stumps and possibly broken up stems from the herbaceous border. The large stems of kale and Brussels sprouts should be well bashed and cut into shorter lengths with an axe. See that the material is nicely moistened —but not swamped. A wet heap will be cold and airless and the breaking-down process hindered.

Over the layer of waste sprinkle a handful of sulphate of ammonia or nitrate of chalk. This will act as an accelerator and start up fermentation. Next place a thin layer of soil. A little hydrated lime can be sprinkled on this. Go on building up in layers in this way until the heap is complete or you have used up all the material. If the heap isn't quite finished cover with some old sacks. A height of 4 ft. is sufficient, when the last layer should be well covered with soil and lightly pressed down. Over this place a covering to keep off rain but see that the covering does not rest directly on the heap. It is unnecessary to shake all the soil from any weeds. A little more soil will be all to the good. After a few weeks the heap should be turned, taking care to place what was the outside of the heap towards the centre and adding more water if needed. Compost made in this way will be ready in about five or six months but will take longer during the winter months. (*Fig. 9.*)

In planning the heap select a spot that is in partial shade. A 3 ft. × 3 ft. or 4 ft. × 4 ft. heap is usually large enough for the small garden. It is better to have two smallish heaps rather than one big one, but too small a heap will not retain the necessary heat.

Many will prefer to use a container or bin of some kind. A useful bin is easily made with rough cuts from a saw mill. These can be nailed to pieces of 2 in. × 2 in. The boards should be given a spacing of 1 in. to admit air. Fig. 10 should make this clear. On no account use sheets of iron as a surround.

Instead of a sprinkling of sulphate of ammonia a proprietary activator can be used as Garotta, Adco, Fertisan etc. and

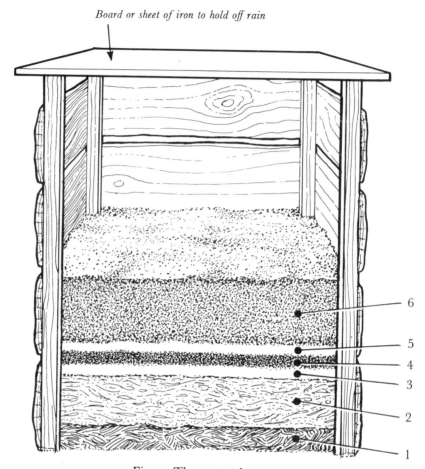

Board or sheet of iron to hold off rain

Fig. 9. The compost heap.

1. Coarse material.
2. 6-in. layer of mixed vegetable waste.
3. Dusting of activator.
4. Thin layer of soil.
5. Sprinkling of lime.
6. 6-in. layer of vegetable waste.
Subsequent layers to height of approx. 4 ft.

there is also a herbal preparation sold as Q.R.—an interesting method for those who object to using chemicals in the garden. This is from a formula devised by Miss Maye E. Bruce.

Another method of composting (and a very sound one) is carried out by using a thin layer of manure between each layer of vegetable waste. Each layer should be covered with a little soil and a dusting of lime. This is known as the Indore process and was evolved by the late Sir Albert Howard. It does, of course, pre-suppose a small amount of manure being available.

Unfortunately there is never enough waste to make sufficient compost but this can be overcome by using some of the humus-forming materials already indicated in a previous chapter. Straw for instance will make a splendid replacement if it is first composted, or alternatively small quantities can be mixed in with any vegetable waste.

Straw must first be thoroughly wetted and this can be a real job. Bales of various sizes can be purchased from any fodder dealer and can be dealt with by first opening up the bale and spreading it out over the ground. A concreted area or a hard wide

Fig. *10. A compost bin made from rough cuts. The front section is not shown.
Boards cut to a suitable length can be slipped in behind the front posts of
2 × 2 as the bin is filled and lifted out to facilitate emptying.*

*Composting straw. Each layer is dusted with an accelerating agent and well wetted. Such material when composted
will be ideal for digging into the soil.*

path is really needed. Spread the straw to a depth of 12 ins. over the area. Straw is covered with a varnish-like substance that renders it almost impervious to water until it is bruised and broken. Just pouring water over it is no good; the water will run through. You must use a fine rose or one of the garden sprinklers. At intervals tread and trample and turn the straw in order to break it up and add more water. Several applications over two or three days will be needed and when the straw has been really wetted the heap can be made. A pair of rubber boots will not come amiss for this job. A large bale of straw will cover quite an area when spread out and you may have to wet half at a time. The other half can be left out for rain to start the wetting process.

The heap is built in the normal way by making 10-in. layers. In order to get a tidy heap make sure that each corner is made firm and then fill up the middle. A light treading should be done in this case. Over each layer of straw apply 3 oz. of sulphate of ammonia and as the heap is built add a layer of soil here and there and dust this with lime. Turning the heap will be necessary once or twice together with re-wetting if it appears to be too dry. It will be ready to dig in as manure in from six to nine months. A complete fertilizer should be given over the surface of the soil and worked in after digging in the composted straw.

As well as vegetable waste from the garden do not forget when seeking material for a compost heap that manure from the fowl run, droppings from sheep and goats and domestic pets, nettles and weeds cut from the roadside will all add to the supply. Many other sources of supply will be found. Kitchen waste in the shape of potato and apple peelings, cabbage and lettuce leaves, pea and bean pods, and faded flowers will all help. But do not include cinders or ash from the domestic boiler or fat and grease. Dry autumn leaves should be composted separately as also should sawdust—both are very slow to rot down.

In theory weed seeds can be composted as the heat generated in the heap should destroy both seeds and disease spores but as the heating up and break-down on the outside of a heap is seldom perfect I prefer not to include certain weeds that have seeded but rather to collect them before they seed. With diseased waste I should consign it to the bonfire with any hard wooded material.

There is another splendid source of humus-forming material that should be mentioned. If you live anywhere near a mushroom farm old mushroom compost can be had and this can be a most useful addition to the soil.

Much more could be written about the use of compost but space does not permit its inclusion. I hope that what little I have been able to write will help those, and there are so many, who find it difficult to get organic replacements of any kind.

A market pack of asparagus. The variety is 'Colossal'.

Photo : Suttons.

A new F_1 variety of summer cabbage— 'Stonehead'. Solid round heads 6 in. across and $5\frac{1}{2}$ in. deep are produced and which will stand for several weeks.

Photo : Dobies.

Savoy cabbage 'Dwarf Green Curled'. A very hardy variety with beautifully curled foliage.

Photo: Dobies.

Brussels Sprouts. Good firm sprouts can only be grown on firm ground. Always pick from the bottom upwards.

Photo: Dobies.

Cauliflower 'Snow Drift' and first heads of Calabrese.
Photo: Dobies.

6 Frames and cloches

Both the garden frame and cloches are invaluable adjuncts to the equipment of any garden and particularly so in the small garden where no greenhouse may be available. The frame may be anything from an elaborate and permanent structure of bricks or concrete or as is more usual, one made of wood and of modest dimensions. Even a reasonably sized box with the bottom removed and the top covered with an odd sheet or two of glass will serve to protect a few seedlings.

It is impossible to mention the varying types and makes of frames for there are many and it must suffice to say that the usual type is one that measures 6 ft. ×4 ft. and this is covered with what is known as the English light. This light is divided by two or three sash bars and glazed with small overlapping panes of glass (*Fig. 11*). This design however can be greatly modified to suit the particular needs of the gardener who may not want a large frame for a number of reasons. There are also metal frames where in most cases the

A 6 × 4 ft. frame with both space- and soil-warming cables. The soil-warming cables are laid 4 to 5 in. below the surface. Photo: Electrical Development Association.

sides as well as the roof are glazed. These admit more light but lose heat more quickly than a brick or wood frame.

Over the last forty years or so another type of light has come to us from the market gardens of Holland. This is the Dutch light and consists of a rectangular wooden frame glazed with one large pane of glass. The overall size of the one shown is 59 in. × 31½ in. (*Fig. 12*).

It is obvious that a heated frame will have advantages over an unheated or cold frame

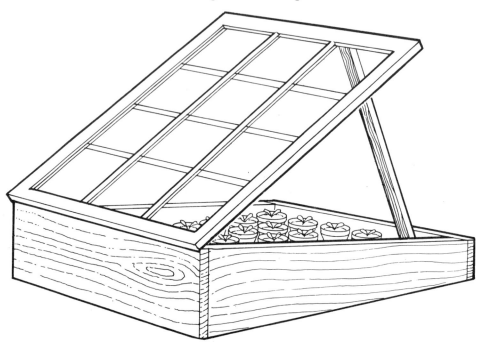

Fig. 11. English 6 × 4 frame and light.

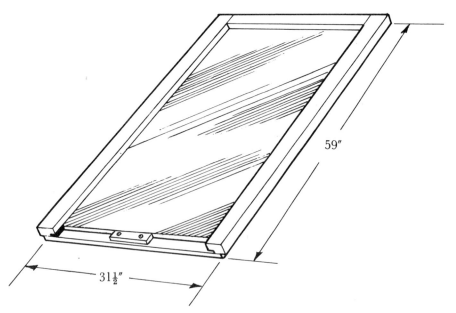

Fig. 12. A Dutch light. The styles and top end are grooved to hold the one large pane of glass which simply slides in and is secured by the stop at the bottom.

but it is not every gardener who will have the facilities for heating a frame, or indeed the need, and in this case the cold frame serves quite well. Crops normally sown in the autumn such as early cauliflowers or onions are overwintered in a cold frame for planting out in the spring. Many crops can be successfully raised and grown in the early spring; early radishes, lettuce, mint, salad onions, carrots, beetroot and turnips can all be sown at much earlier dates than they could in the open and the crops gathered and enjoyed correspondingly early. During the summer months such crops as cucumbers and melons can occupy the frame. These few crops by no means exhaust the possi-

bilities of the frame and many other uses will be found during the year.

Cloches are a common sight in many gardens and allotments today and a fresh design seems to spring up every few months. Some are extremely good and stay the course while others soon disappear from the market.

Of the glass cloches there are three main types—the tent, the barn and a flat-top cloche. The tent is usually 2 ft. long with a span of approximately 10 in. The barn—by far the best type—is 2 ft. long and 22 in. wide, with side walls of 6, 9 or 12 in. high, permitting room for several rows of the smaller growing subjects (turnips, carrots

The I.C.I. polythene tunnel. The 35-ft. length of polythene can be made into three 10-ft. lengths or as shown into two 15-ft. lengths. Supporting hoops and wires are supplied with the polythene. Photo: Messrs Imperial Chemical Industries Ltd.

etc.) and two rows of larger plants. Tomatoes would need the whole area.

With the advent of plastic materials many new designs of cloche have been introduced and the merits of glass versus polythene freely argued. Polythene or other plastic material has the advantage over glass of being very light to handle, but this lightness makes them very vulnerable to winds unless they are firmly anchored. Most patterns now provide in their design long extensions of the wires that can be pushed well down into the soil. They are a little cheaper to buy than the glass cloches but the plastic material will need renewing from time to time. Owing to surface tension, condensation does not run off in droplets as easily as with glass and some light is screened off under these conditions. Nevertheless polythene cloches are very worth while and where one is scared of glass in the garden they can be recommended so long as plenty of air is given.

The reader will probably have seen in the strawberry growing districts long tunnels, covering rows of strawberries to encourage early fruiting. These tunnels can be had in short lengths suitable for the small garden together with hoops over which the polythene is draped and wires to hold it in place. A 35-ft. row can be purchased from most garden shops and this can be made to provide two shorter rows of 15 ft.

What has been said about crops for the cold frame can in general be said about cloches. Cloches have one advantage over the garden frame in that they fit into the normal procedure of gardening as regards sowing and planting. The usual long rows can be sown or planted and protected with cloches until such time as weather conditions permit the cloches to be moved. The crop can then be grown on in the normal way. Meanwhile the cloches should be put to further use by setting them over another sowing or planting.

Although there is no reason why cloches should not be used to give protection to any sowings or planting that may need coverage, they should be used continuously in time as well as in space and to get the utmost from them a small section of the garden should be set aside especially for cloche crops. A narrow strip of ground 6 ft. wide will give ample space for two positions of a row of cloches and a path. To use glass or any protective material to the full means that you will be more intensive in your cropping. While this means more produce from a given area it also means that the extra nourishment the plants will require must be supplied. A small strip can be maintained at a high degree of fertility with replacements of humus-forming material and fertilizers more easily than the whole garden and such a soil, rich in humus, will be more retentive of moisture which will be ideal for cloche crops (*Fig. 13*).

A strip of this kind will also save labour in carrying the cloches from one place to another in the garden. As cropping proceeds the cloches need only be moved sideways from one position to the other—a matter of just over 2 ft. If protection for odd sowings in another part of the garden is needed a few more cloches or a tunnel will be required.

You do of course need to have some idea in mind as to what you are to grow and a simple succession should be planned that will carry you through the year. One thing to bear in mind in planning is that when one of your favourite crops must occupy the ground for the whole year or the greater part of the year, you will need a third position; a row of asparagus or strawberries for instance. Here is a simple rotation that does not include a permanent crop:

	Position 1		*Position 2*
1.	Lettuce	2.	Dwarf beans
	C. Oct.–Apr.		C. Apr.–Late May
	Cut Apr.–May		Pick July
3.	Frame cucumbers	4.	Late lettuce
	C. June–Sept.		C. late Sept.–Nov.
	Cut Aug.–Sept.		Sow in the open in Aug.
			Cut Oct.–Nov.
5.	Peas or beans		
	C. Nov.–March		

C = Cloched period

See also Fig. 14

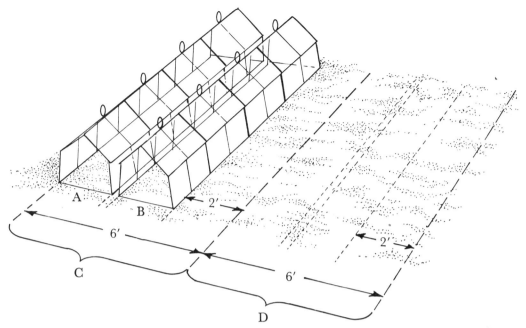

Fig. 13. Two-strip cropping. A strip 6 ft. wide allows two positions for one row of cloches for continuous cropping. The cloches are moved from A to B and B to A as cropping demands. Double rows can be used on each 6-ft. strip and both rows moved to and from C and D as needed thus using a 12-ft. strip.

	Crop	Oct	Nov	Dec	Jan	Feb	Mar	Apr	May	Jun	Jul	Aug	Sep
1st position	Lettuce												
2nd position	Dwarf beans												
1st position	Cucumbers												
2nd position	Lettuce												
1st position	Peas or beans												

☐☐☐☐☐ Period cloched

────── Total period occupied by crop

Fig. 14. A simple two-strip rotation for cloches.

In a small book on vegetable growing one can only touch on the fringe of intensive work with frames and cloches but if you are interested you would find my book *Growing Under Glass* helpful.

It is surprising that cloches are not used in northern districts to a greater extent than they are. The northern gardener would be able to make many sowings several weeks earlier than would otherwise be the case and thus extend the all-too-short season of growth; in industrial areas cloches do much

The ends of cloche rows must always be closed. The photograph shows the end of a row of Chase barn cloches being closed with a pane of glass. Photo: Messrs Expandite Ltd.

to protect young plants from impurities in the atmosphere. For the earliest sowings the cloches should be put into position a week or even two weeks previous to sowing in order to warm up and dry the surface of the soil and thus assist germination. Always remember that the ends of the row should be closed; open ends may turn the cloches into a wind tunnel and also leave the rows open to the birds. Cats love to get under them where they find a warm soil to lie on, and thus damaging young plants.

In thinking of cloches remember that by using them the season of growth can be extended both in the early spring and in the autumn. Sowings can therefore be made at a much earlier date and the harvest carried over until a late date in the autumn, thus enabling many crops to be available when similar crops without protection have succumbed to adverse weather.

A number of subjects are specially suitable for frame and cloch cultivation but instead of dealing with them in this section notes on the cultivation of these vegetables will be found later in this book under the heading of the vegetable concerned, thus saving tiresome repetitions. Under *Lettuce* for instance will be found a note on frame and cloche culture.

7 The Culture of Vegetables

The only way to produce good vegetables is by careful and painstaking husbandry. To imagine that any magic potion will compensate for lack of preparation or attention is to court disaster and disappointment. To start off with a well-prepared site is half the battle towards success; the rest will depend on a wise selection of seeds from a reliable source and careful attention to the needs of the plants.

It is impossible to give a long list of varieties. Those mentioned are intended as a general guide. For a greater selection of varieties the reader should consult the attractively illustrated lists sent out by seedsmen each year.

In planning the following chapters on the cultivation of vegetables likely to be needed it became a question as to whether it would be more convenient to deal with each in alphabetical order or to adopt some method of grouping and deal with each group under a common heading such as 'The Cabbage Family'. The latter seemed to be the better and more interesting approach and allows what would be a very long section to be divided into smaller groups.

PEAS AND BEANS

Peas. If you have never eaten young and well-grown peas from the garden you have no idea what fresh and well-flavoured peas can taste like. The garden pea is undoubtedly one of the most popular of all vegetables and the first dish is eagerly looked forward to by most households. Peas can be well grown on most soils provided they are deeply worked and fertile but they do need a lot of attention and take up a lot of room if more than one row is to be grown.

Peas fall into two groups: (1) round-seeded, which are hardier and earlier than (2) wrinkled or marrowfat. The latter are better flavoured as they have a higher sugar content. For the autumn or the earliest spring sowings the round-seeded varieties are sown, followed by one or more of the marrowfat varieties.

In preparing the ground, double-digging should be done, for peas are deep rooters and dung or compost should go into the second spit as well as the top spit. A dusting of lime should be given and later, before sowing, give a dressing of superphosphate at roughly 1 oz. per square yard.

The first sowing is made in early or mid-November or in early February and in colder districts the first sowing may have to wait until early March, for nothing will be gained by sowing until the ground is fit to work. Gardeners in colder districts would do well to cover the first sowing with cloches as this would permit earlier sowing to be done with safety. These first sowings should be one of the round-seeded varieties.

A sowing of a wrinkled variety is often made in late February or March to closely follow the autumn or early February sowing and in April one of the maincrop varieties is sown. Where space permits, a succession giving supplies from May to September can be contrived and a sowing is made just as soon as a previous sowing is well through the ground. In small gardens where space is limited the gardener must rely on two or possibly three sowings, choosing the more dwarf varieties. Where cloche protection can be given a dwarf variety is best as it can remain cloched for a longer period. In many gardens a sowing is made of an early variety in mid-June to provide a late picking in September.

A rewarding crop of peas. Photo: Messrs Sutton & Sons Ltd.

Mice are liable to destroy the hopes of an early crop of peas unless traps are set to catch them.

It is usual to sow peas in a wide flat drill taken out with a draw hoe. The drill should be 2 to 3 in. deep. Sow the seed evenly over the whole of the drill and aim at dropping the seed at 2 in. apart each way. Of course, you won't do this but you could try. In any case do not sow too thickly. For later sowings draw the drill a little deeper and do not completely fill it in after sowing so that the surface will remain a little below the surrounding soil. This will facilitate watering later on during the summer.

When several rows of peas are being grown it must be remembered that they must be well spaced and it is the usual practice to allow half the total height on either side of the row. With tall varieties a low-growing crop can occupy the ground as a catch crop.

Mice are very apt to steal the seed and it is necessary to take some steps to prevent this happening especially with the early sowings. The seed can be rolled in a paste of red lead and paraffin but it is a messy business and I prefer to set traps along the rows. If you do this do not forget to keep the traps set and baited or you may find a neat row of holes all along the drill where the mice have been after the seed.

Staking can be rather a problem today as the pea boughs we used to buy are not so easily obtained but they are just the thing if you can get them. In any case it is better to give even the little plants enough support to prevent them falling over and this can be done by way of very short twiggy sticks from the hedgerows. This should be done even if the row is cloched. Later on, additional support must be given even with the dwarf varieties and a very good substitute for stakes is netting which can be purchased from most garden shops. This should be placed along each side of the rows and firmly supported.

Hoeing should be done regularly alongside the rows and the tendency should be to draw the soil towards the plants. The area between the plants will have to be hand weeded. Annual weeds can make a thick wet

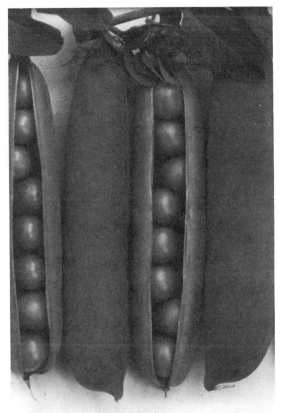

Garden pea, Sutton's 'Sweetness'. The first wrinkled-seeded pea to mature as early as a round-seeded variety. A very heavy cropper. Photo: Messrs Sutton & Sons Ltd.

Pods of garden pea, 'Onward'. A splendid variety for the small garden as well as the market grower. Photo: Messrs Sutton & Sons Ltd.

mass round the young peas and encourage mildew. Peas are thirsty subjects and they will need plenty of water. A mulch after a good watering will help to conserve moisture.

When picking use both hands. Hold the stem of the plant with one hand and snap off the pod with the other. Leave the basket on the ground so that you have both hands free.

Peas and beans have the power to add nitrogen to the soil and the roots should be left and dug in when the crop has been cleared.

Cloches are a great help with early peas. The autumn sowing can be cloched until such a time in the spring that they nearly reach the top of a small cloche (usually in March) when they can be decloched and properly staked or larger cloches used and

grown on almost to maturity if the variety is a dwarf one. Cloches are also used for the February sowings.

In the south very late picking can be had by sowing in mid-July and cloching the row in mid-September.

Suggested varieties

EARLIES

C. Meteor. R. 12–15 in. tall. Very dwarf and the hardiest of the early peas.

C. Feltham First. R. 18 in. Blunt-ended pods in pairs. Very early.

C. Kelvedon Wonder. W. 18 in. Excellent for both early and late sowing and resistant to mildew.

C indicates suitable for early cloched sowings.

R indicates round-seeded.
W indicates wrinkled-seeded.

SECOND EARLY OR EARLY MAINCROP

Onward. W. 2½ ft. A most popular variety and very prolific. Often seen on the show bench.

Hurst Green Shaft. W. 2½ ft. A newer variety with triple pods. Resistant to mildew.

Achievement. W. 4–5 ft. A splendid cropper and of exhibition value.

MAINCROP

Lord Chancellor. W. 4 ft. An excellent maincrop variety with pointed pods. Well flavoured and prolific.

Alderman. W. A well-tried old variety. A very heavy cropper.

Senator. W. A grand cropper with handsome medium green pods in pairs.

There are several varieties popular on the Continent and grown to some extent in this country:

The asparagus pea. Quite distinct from normal types but the main feature is the rectangular winged pods and reddish flowers. Dwarf in habit and only needs short stakes.

The sugar pea. (Mangetout). An excellent edible-podded pea with a very sweet flavour. They are simply topped and tailed like French beans.

Petit pois. The small-seeded French pea. Very sweet and of good flavour. Dwarf in habit.

The pods of all these must be gathered while still young and small. The pods are cooked whole. Sowings can be made in April or May.

Broad beans. The three types of broad beans grown are: (1) long-pod, which may be either white or green seeded; (2) broad-podded or Windsor varieties, which are also white or green seeded; and (3) small-podded varieties, which are either tall or dwarf. The long-pods are hardier and therefore the most suitable for autumn or early spring sowing. They give the heaviest of yields and there is little to choose between one good strain and another, but you do need to know whether it

is a green or a white seeded variety if you have any preference. Windsors are not so attractive in appearance and beings less hardy than longpods are sown later. The flavour however is much superior.

The small-podded varieties are well worth growing especially where space is limited. The dwarf varieties take up much less room and produce a very large number of small pods. Being very dwarf they are particularly suitable for sowing under cloches. It is just a question of whether it is worth while growing the taller small-podded kinds as the yield is poor.

While peas are difficult to grow properly, broad beans are just the opposite. They form one of the easiest of crops to grow and are not at all choosy as regards soil. The earliest of sowings are made in mid-October or November or in early February as soon as the ground can be worked.

The ground should be dug and manured some time ahead of sowing and before the seed is sown a dressing of superphosphate (3 oz. to each square yard) should be worked into the surface together with a little sulphate of potash (1 oz. per square yard). The best way to sow is to take out two drills 6–7 in. apart and 3 in. deep. The seed is dropped into each drill at staggered intervals of 6 in. and covered in. Autumn sowings can be covered with small cloches to ensure a safe passage through the winter. A similar sowing can be made in late January or early February and cloches will help to ensure quick and even germination. Further sowings may be made in March or April using either one of the longpods or a Windsor variety.

The small-podded varieties are also sown in March. These too are conveniently sown in double rows as described but the seeds can be dropped at 6 in. apart. Where more than one double row is to be sown they should be 2 ft. 6 in. apart but the small-pods need only 18 in.

Where for various reasons early sowings cannot be made outside, the seed can be sown in boxes and the plants raised in the frame and transplanted to the open garden when weather permits.

Before covering in the drills sow a dozen

Broad beans, Sutton's 'White Eye'. A white-seeded variety that produces a huge crop of medium-sized pods. Photo: Messrs Sutton & Sons Ltd.

or so extra seeds at the end of the row. You may need them to fill any gaps later on.

Hoe through the crop regularly and remove any basal shoots from the longpods and pinch out the growing point of the plant as soon as four or five clusters of blooms are out. This will help the early development of the pods and also do much to discourage the dreaded black fly. If any signs of the pest are seen they must be dealt with at once.

Gather the pods while they are still young. A test can be made by opening up a pod, when the bean should still be soft. If left too long the 'eye' will become black, the skin will be tough and the bean mealy and hard.

Suggested varieties

Long-pods. Aquadulce. Colossal.

Windsors. Giant Windsor. Harlington Green or Harlington White.

Small-pods. The Sutton. Dwarf Fan.

Runner beans. There can be few gardens or allotments in which runner beans are not grown and one cannot help noticing that even while the rest of the garden may be sadly neglected there will be a row of runner beans. Indeed, the runner seems to be a long-suffering plant for under the most unlikely conditions it will produce a crop of sorts. But if you want a bountiful return a good deal of work must go into the preparation of the soil and some after-care must follow. A well-grown row will provide the family with an abundance of this popular vegetable over a long period. A row of 25 ft. is quite capable of yielding 1 cwt. of pods.

Unfortunately runners are frost-tender and unprotected sowings should not be made until the third week in May in the south: in colder districts late May or early June. The site should be double-dug as with peas and the second spit as well as the first should be well manured. Some gardeners prefer to take out a trench in the autumn and put into the bottom plenty of vegetable waste and in the spring fill up the trench with rich soil. On the whole a 3-ft. strip double-dug, with the third spit loosened, plus plenty of manure in the top two spits, will provide a better root run. When manuring, use a large barrow-load of dung or compost to 10 square yards plus a dressing of a complete fertilizer (3 oz. to the square yard). This should be worked into the top few inches a few days before sowing.

Runners are usually sown in two rows 12 in. apart and the seed spaced at 9 in. along each drill in opposite positions. This will fit in with the normal method of staking later on. Sow the seed 2–2½ in. deep. The sowing is often made in a shallow and wide trench, which greatly facilitates watering during the drier months and provides quarters for a mulch. This is important, for if the plants become dry at the roots, bud dropping is bound to occur. Ample water will be needed and the mulch will help to maintain the moist root run that the plants demand.

Runners, like broad beans, are sometimes sown in a box and given frame protection until planting out can be safely effected. This must of course wait until all fear of frost has passed.

Support of some kind must be given for the plants to twine round. If you can get them,

Runner bean, 'Hammond's Dwarf Scarlet'. A true form of runner. It is early and needs no staking. Photo: Messrs W. J. Unwin Ltd.

A grand row of runner beans. Photo: Messrs Sutton & Sons Ltd.

chestnut poles of 8 ft. are ideal, otherwise alternative support will have to be given. Large pea boughs are often used, or wire and string strongly supported at each end of the row with posts is another possibility (*Fig. 15*). Runners can be grown 'dwarfed' by pinching out the growing point when the shoot is a foot high and keeping the resultant side shoots pinched but it is better to let the plants climb. In any case pinch out the tips

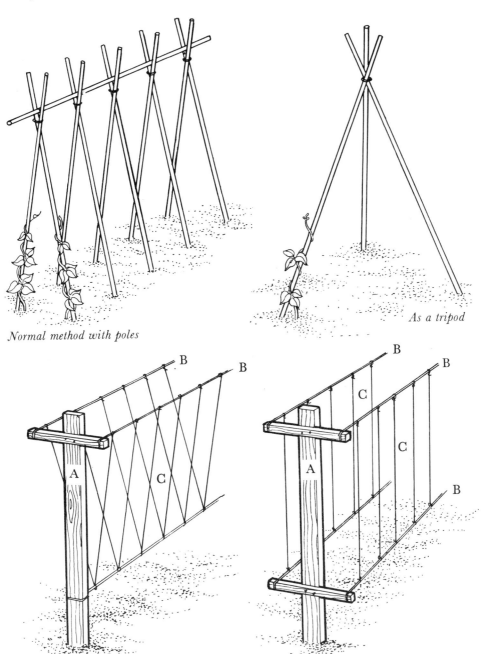

Normal method with poles

As a tripod

Fig. 15. Methods of supporting runner beans.
    A. Posts at end of rows.
    B. Wire.
    C. Stout filler.

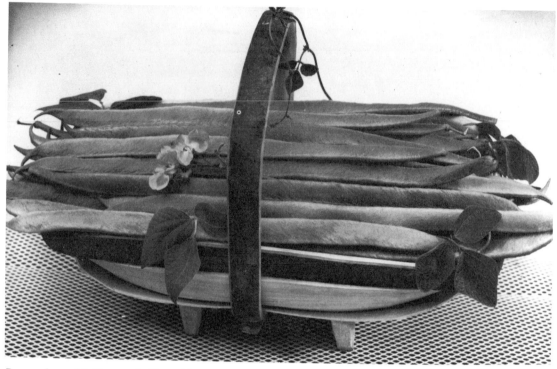

Runner bean, 'Achievement' (Sutton's). An outstanding runner for colour and length of pod. A superb variety for showing. Photo: Messrs Sutton & Sons Ltd.

when the shoots reach the top of the support.

Runners should be picked and eaten while they are still young. Unless you want beans a yard long for the show bench there is no merit in growing those monstrous long pods. They are often coarse and need much more preparation in the kitchen. Pick regularly and never allow the pods to become old and 'beany'.

Where an early dish is needed a sowing can be made about mid-April under cloches. The plants must remain covered until frosts are no longer expected, when the cloches can be removed and the plants given support. When the family consists of two or three persons and only small pickings are needed a good plan is to sow half of the row in mid-April with an early variety such as Kelvedon Wonder or Princeps and sow the other half of the row early in June in the normal way. A supply would then be available in small quantities from mid-July until frosts cut the plants down.

Good varieties

Kelvedon Wonder (Early)

Enorma (Twenty-One)

Achievement

Hammond's Dwarf Scarlet. A true dwarf runner that needs no support.

Dwarf French or kidney beans. Dwarf beans should be more extensively grown than they are for they are easy to grow, occupy little space and are earlier and of superior flavour than the runner. Strains today are far in advance of those offered years ago and stringless or snap-podded, a feature of modern strains. Dwarf beans are a little hardier than their cousin, the runner, but they must not be sown outdoors until mid-April. Successional sowings can be made until July.

Dwarf beans thrive best in rich deep soil moderately manured. A dressing comprising superphosphate of lime 2 parts and sulphate of potash 1 part should be given and worked into the top few inches a few days before sowing.

If the soil is too cold and wet to sow it is better to wait until conditions improve or the seed may rot. An early sowing can be

A favourite dwarf French bean, 'The Prince'. Photo: Messrs Sutton & Sons Ltd.

An occasional syringing over with water during hot weather will be appreciated by dwarf beans and will also discourage red spider. An early crop under barn cloches. Photo: Messrs Expandite Ltd.

made under cloches early in April if the site is cloched a week or ten days beforehand. This will ensure good soil conditions. Sowings can also be made in a box 4½ in. deep as suggested for runners and the box can be placed in the garden frame until some time in May when the plants can be set outdoors.

Sowing should be done in a double row, dropping two seeds at staggered intervals of 8 or 9 in. and 2 in. deep. When the little plants are some 3 or 4 in. high, pull out the weaker of the two. A few extra seeds at the end of the row will ensure replacements if needed.

Very little attention is needed beside weeding and watering, but before the plants become heavy with pods some short twiggy stakes should be placed among the plants or they may be blown over by wind or beaten down by heavy rain. In the latter event the pods might become muddy and useless.

The season of cropping is shorter than with runners and if a continuity of supply is needed successional sowings should be made. Failure to keep the pods gathered will lessen the period of cropping.

Varieties

The Prince. One of the earliest to mature and an immense cropper. Almost stringless.
Masterpiece. A little later than The Prince but one of the finest dwarfs introduced. Bears an immense crop of long pods.
The Sprite. A stringless variety of outstanding merit. A round- or pencil-podded variety, the pods being short and almost cylindrical.
Granda. An older and well-known stringless variety.
Mont d'or (Golden Butter). Pods long and stringless and of a golden colour.
Comtesse de Chambord. A dual-purpose bean bearing later than normal. The pods can be eaten green or allowed to ripen and the small white seeds stored for use as a haricot.

8 Root crops

The ideal soil for root crops is a deep sandy loam but unfortunately we cannot all cultivate on such a soil and we must work down the soil available to as deep and fine a state as possible, because good and well-shaped roots cannot be grown on lumpy and stony ground. On the heavier soils the addition of sharp sand and peat, not ashes, and thorough forking and raking will help to reduce the soil to a much finer texture. Root crops should be grown on soil that has been generously manured for a previous crop. The addition of any fresh animal manure will cause the roots to fork badly and on previously manured ground all that is necessary is to give a dressing of some complete fertilizer before sowing.

Roots fall into three types in accordance with the length of the roots, which may be long, medium or short. It is impossible to grow the long tapering roots on anything but light and very deeply worked soil but the intermediate or short types will do quite well on the more shallow soils. In any case the long tapering roots of parsnips and carrots seen on the show bench will be severely curtailed by the cook and the large beetroot are often coarse and as they cannot be cut back, a very large saucepan is needed in which to cook them. So for good reasons the intermediate types are better to grow for store, while the short-rooted kinds find favour for early and more immediate use.

If you want the long type of carrot or parsnip for exhibition you will need to prepare special stations by making deep holes with a crowbar. The holes should be 3 ft. deep and 3–4 in. in diameter and filled with a good potting compost.

Beetroot. The soil for beetroot should be dug in the autumn or well ahead of sowing time and in the spring forked through and reduced to the fine tilth needed. A few days before sowing give a dressing of some complete fertilizer at about 4 oz. to the square yard. If you want to mix your own fertilizer the formula given on page 22 can be used. The beetroot family hails from the seaside and the plants will benefit from a dressing of salt applied once or twice along the rows during the growing season. One ounce of salt to a yard run is sufficient.

The earliest sowings can be made in the frame or under cloches towards the end of March using one of the early globe types. At the end of March sowings can be made on a warm border in the southern districts. Otherwise sowings should not be made until well into April and in May for a summer crop and for storing. Successional sowings of an early globe can be made until late June.

Sow in drills 12 to 15 in. apart. The drills should be 1 in. deep and the seed thinly sown. What is known as the seed is really a capsule that may contain from two to six seeds. Cover in the drills and lightly firm as described in a previous chapter. When the seedlings are large enough thin out until the little plants stand at 6 in. apart. In the north and on heavy ground it may not be possible to sow until mid-May without protection as the little seedlings are liable to frost damage.

The small roots for salads should always be used while quite young and pulled when they are little bigger than golf balls. The secret of obtaining these tender young roots is to grow them without a check. If any check occurs through dryness of the soil the plants are very liable to run to seed. To avoid bleeding always twist off the leaves. Do not cut them off.

A good job of digging. Note that the left hand is placed palm downwards and the right hand used as a lever pushing downwards when lifting the soil.

Photo: L.N.F.

A good crop of early peas. The variety is 'Forward', a round variety with a better flavour than most early peas.

Photo: Unwins.

A splendid main-crop pea 'Onward'. The blunt-ended pods hang in pairs.

Photo: Unwins.

Turnip 'Green Top Stone'. The flesh is white and the flavour mild. Suitable for main crop.

Photo: Unwins.

Carrot 'Early Nantes'. A useful and reliable variety for early work.

Photo: Unwins.

'Chantenay'—a valuable half-long carrot suitable for the main crop for storing.

Photo: Unwins.

Turnip 'Golden Ball'. A yellow flesh turnip that stands the hard weather well. Good variety for late sowing.

Photo: Unwins.

Beetroot, 'Detroit Globe'. Deep red in colour and free from rings. Photo : Messrs W. J. Unwin Ltd.

Varieties suggested

Detroit Selected Globe. Early and a fine deep red and free from rings.

Covent Garden. A well-known variety for late use and storing. An intermediate type.

Cheltenham Green Top. A long beet widely grown where large roots are wanted.

Perpetual or spinach beet. The leaves of this variety form an excellent substitute for spinach.

Carrots. Like beetroot, carrots have long been an important vegetable crop and owing to their high vitamin value are even more popular today than ever. Many of the short and stump-rooted varieties were introduced by the French gardeners, varieties we still use and value such as French Forcing, Early Nantes, Chantenay etc. As with other roots small or medium types have become more popular than the long types, which require such deep soils.

The preparation of the soil must be carried out as for beet but with carrots fanging or forking is easily brought about by lumpy or stony soil.

Carrots for storing are usually sown in early May or even early June and harvested at the end of October. For early and summer use, the seed can be sown from early March until July. Very early pullings are had by sowing in early February in the frame or under cloches using one of the early types such as Short Horn or Amsterdam Forcing. Successional sowings should be made to provide a continuity of supply. For storing, one of the intermediate varieties should be sown.

The seed is small and should not be sown too deeply. Shallow drills $\frac{1}{2}$ to $\frac{3}{4}$ in. should be drawn out and the seed sown in a continuous row. The rows should be spaced at 12 in. apart. A little silver sand mixed with the seed will help to achieve thin sowing.

If the seed is sown thinly initially, little thinning will be necessary later with the earliest varieties, but the seedlings must not be allowed to crowd each other. Later, little roots can be pulled when they are just big enough to cook or use in a salad. At this stage they are delicious. Those left will have room to grow on. Main crop sowings will need to be thinned to about 6 in. depending on the variety. Needless to say the rows should be kept free from weeds by frequent use of the hoe.

Under frames and cloches carrots can be enjoyed at a very early date. Have the cloches in position on prepared ground some 10 or 14 days before sowing. This will not only warm the ground to some extent but dry the surface and make the final preparations possible. Prepare the soil in the frame and put the 'light' in position. Sowings can be done early in February or even late January in the south but rather later in the more exposed districts. The rows can be as close as 6 in. in the frame and three or four can be sown under barn cloches. The cloches or frame lights can be removed early in April. The seed is often broadcast in the frame and raked in and lightly firmed.

The great enemy of carrots is the carrot fly. This will not worry the early sowings as the carrots will be used before the female fly gets busy egg-laying. For later sowings it is as well to assume that the crop will be attacked and to take precautions. Always re-firm the soil after thinning and remove any thinnings rather than leave them between the rows. The scent will attract the fly. (See Pests and Diseases, chapter 18.)

Varieties

Early Gem. Early and suitable for sowing

Turnip, 'Selected Early Snowball'. An excellent variety for early summer. Photo: Messrs W. J. Unwin Ltd.

in frames or under cloches. Roots 3–4 in. long.

Early Nantes. Early and suitable for sowing in frames or under cloches. A blunt-ended root of excellent colour. A little longer than Early Gem and useful for successional sowings.

Chantenay. Probably the most popular of the intermediate type.

Long Red Surrey. An old variety with very long straight roots of good colour.

Turnips. Here is another vegetable that is grown for its high food value and can be had right through the year. The green tops can be eaten as 'greens' and they are a great favourite with dieticians because the vitamin content is said to be the highest of any vegetable.

There are two main types of turnips, early and maincrop. The early turnips are those specially suitable for frame work and for early and successional sowings outdoors. These early varieties all have round or spherical roots and are sown from early spring until late summer. They mature quickly and do not keep. Maincrop turnips are sown in the early summer for winter storage. They mature more slowly and can be left in the ground and pulled as needed throughout the winter in the more southern districts but in colder and more exposed areas the roots are lifted in the autumn and clamped or stored in boxes with sand in a cool place.

If you are lucky enough to have a heated frame a first sowing can be made of one of the frame varieties at the end of January or under cloches at the end of February. Towards the end of March a sowing can be made in the south on a warm border, again using one of the early varieties. As with all the roots it is best to sow on a site that was well manured for a previous crop and the top 4 or 5 in. should be worked down to as fine a tilth as possible. A liberal dressing of peat plus a general fertilizer will provide a good medium for quick growth. It is essential that turnips, especially the early ones, should be grown without check or they will become 'woody' and unpleasant. Any dryness will bring about a check and until the seedlings are well established they should be given water if the weather is dry.

Sowing is done in the normal way in shallow V-shaped drills $\frac{1}{2}$ to $\frac{3}{4}$ in. deep and 12 in. apart. Gradually thin out to 4 in. apart and pull the roots when they are golfball size. They are delicious at that stage. In the

A promising crop of early turnips under cloches. The variety is 'Early White Milan'.

Turnip, 'Extra Early Milan'. Very suitable for early sowings in frames or under cloches. Photo: Messrs W. J. Unwin Ltd.

frame the rows can be as close as 6 in. apart and under barn cloches two or three rows can be sown.

The main crop is usually sown during May. Turnips do not mind some shade and they can be sown between taller-growing crops such as peas. Maincrop turnips need rather wider spacing and 15 in. between the rows and 9 to 12 in. between the plants will be needed according to variety. Do not forget that swede turnips make excellent eating. These should be sown in May and when ready can be stored or left in the ground.

The chief pest encountered is the Turnip flea beetle or turnip fly as it is more commonly called. The beetle eats out small holes all over the leaves and attacks the seedlings as soon as they appear above ground. There are a number of well-known dodges to deter the flies; dusting with weathered soot while the dew is still on the leaves is helpful but more drastic measures are often needed. An effective gadget is to freshly paint the underside of a board or cover it with grease and pass this over the rows just high enough to clear the leaves. Runners on either side will hold the board above the seedlings and a piece of hessian draped over the front will disturb the beetles which jump up and stick to the wet paint (*Fig. 16*). Dusting with derris will also prove effective if carried out at intervals.

Varieties

Frame: Sutton's Gem.

Cloche and early sowings: Early White Milan.

For use during the summer: Jersey Lily or Green Top Globe.

For Winter use: Manchester Market.

Swede: Purple Top (yellow flesh).

Parsnip. Parsnips are not one of the most popular of vegetables. It may be because it is usually served 'plain boiled' when it does seem to be a poor thing. There are other ways of cooking and serving it, which render it more tasty. Par-boiled and fried in beef dripping or baked round the meat it makes a more interesting vegetable. It is one of the easiest vegetables to grow so long as it has a deep soil. No fresh manure should be added to the soil but the mixture suggested for other

Fig. 16. Home-made trap for turnip flea beetles.
A. Board. Underside wet paint or grease.
B. Hessian to disturb the beetles.

roots will do equally well for parsnips.

Seeds are sown quite early in the year, towards the end of February in the south and as soon as weather and soil conditions permit in the more exposed regions. The rows should be 18 in. apart and the drills 1 to 2 in. in depth according to the type of soil. As the rate of germination is not as high as most other vegetables rather thicker sowing may be done.

Thin out the seedlings as soon as they are an inch or so high and finally leave the plants at 8 in. apart. Where long straight roots are needed for the show bench holes should be bored as mentioned for carrots and filled with a good potting compost. Sow four or five seeds at each station and thin out leaving only the most promising, stronger-looking seedlings.

Although the traditional date for sowing parsnips is February, the soil is often not fit to work at that time, and sowing must wait. This need not bother you, for though it is true that parsnips need a long season of growth, they will still get it if they are not sown until late March and the ground will be warmer and kinder and germination and growth quicker.

Parsnips are usually left in the ground until needed but it is better to lift a few roots in early December in case hard frost makes it impossible to lift them when needed. In February they should however be lifted, the leaves cut off and the roots stored in a shed. Cover the roots with sand or dry earth.

Varieties suggested

Tender and True. A rather shorter variety and of excellent flavour.

The Student. A long and large variety much favoured in the north.

Parsnip, 'Tender and True'. An old and popular variety. Photo: Messrs Sutton & Sons Ltd.

9 Leaf and stalk

Asparagus. Asparagus is regarded as a luxury crop but if the gardener has room for a row or two, can spare the ground, and also feels like tackling a rather tough bit of work he will be rewarded with a supply of this delicious vegetable and earn the envy of every other gardener in the neighbourhood. It must, however, be borne in mind that it is very much a permanent crop and once a bed has been put down it will last twenty years or more and may still be producing a good crop when the owner has departed this life. But it is not a crop for a small garden. A bed of asparagus will not push up its shoots all at one time but throw up shoots here and there over a long period so that for even a small family a considerable number of plants will be needed to ensure a worthwhile quantity at one cut.

Asparagus should not be cut until the plants are four years old. You can sow seeds, and this is the cheapest way, but you will have to wait for four years before you can sample the buds. Obviously the best way is to purchase three-year-old plants and be content with a limited cut the following spring.

The bed must be prepared some time in advance of planting, which should be during April. Because the bed will last a good many years it is well worth making a thorough job of site preparation. It should be free from any water-logging and double-dug. Work in a liberal dressing of manure or the best of the compost into each spit plus a 3 oz. per square yard dressing of bone meal. Wild asparagus is found on the sandy seashore and so does better on a sandy loam than on a clay soil. Where the drainage is good and the soil light a raised bed is not necessary but on a heavier soil every effort must be made to lighten and open up the soil by working in old mortar rubble, coarse grit and sharp sand; anything in fact to help keep the soil open. Throw up soil from each side of the bed thus making a raised bed which will tend to be warmer and better drained. When the bed is finished give a dressing of hydrated lime and leave further work until March, at which time the top 8 or 9 in. should be forked through and the soil worked down to a fine tilth. At the same time work in a 3-oz. dressing per square yard of bone meal.

A convenient size for an asparagus bed is 3 ft. wide with a 2-ft. alleyway on either side so that work can be carried out from either side without getting on the bed. Each bed will take two rows of plants or crowns set at 18 in. apart and 9 in. from the edges. Having ordered the plants take out two trenches 9 in. wide along the bed and approximately 9 in. deep and make a ridge along the centre of the trenches. The depth of the trench and the height of the ridge should be such that the crown when covered will be 4–5 in. below the surface of the bed. The reason for this is that asparagus plants have long and spidery roots which must be well spread out and the plants can be placed astride the ridge and the roots conveniently spread on either side.

The plants will come to you well packed in damp moss and must on no account be allowed to become dry. So have everything ready in good time so that the plants can be unpacked right away and planted. Expose the plants for as little time as possible, covering in as each one is set, and see that they are well firmed.

Many gardeners now prefer to grow the plants in single rows on the flat but the initial preparation must be equally thorough. A space of 2 ft. should be left on either side of the row. In the late autumn when the plants are tidied up a low mound of soil is drawn up over the row and levelled out after cutting.

The beds should be kept free from weeds and hoed through from time to time. In the autumn the fern-like leaves will turn yellow, when they should be cut down to the ground, the bed cleaned up and any spilled soil in the alleyways returned to the bed, the whole being left neat and tidy, a process known by old gardeners as 'tucking in'. A liberal mulch of stable or farmyard manure should have been given over the bed originally but now we must rely on whatever manure we can get, plus any compost that we can spare In early March a mixture consisting of superphosphate of lime 4 parts, sulphate of potash 1 part and sulphate of ammonia 1 part is recommended. This should be well mixed and applied at the rate of 3 oz. per square yard and the bed pricked over with a fork to the depth of 2 in. to loosen up the surface.

Do not be tempted to cut until the plants are four years old and make this a moderate cut. Cutting should be done when the buds are approximately 4 in. above the ground. Cut with a sharp pointed knife or one of the special tools that are available for this job. Thrust the knife into the ground as near to the bud as possible, taking care not to damage nearby buds. Cutting should cease towards the end of June when the 'fern' should be left to grow and nourish the plants. The stems of the foliage are somewhat brittle and in exposed gardens some support by way of pea boughs is helpful otherwise the stems may snap off. Pick up any berries that may fall on the ground or unwanted seedlings will spring up between the plants.

On established beds it is possible to have an early cut by covering part of the bed with cloches in January. Cutting may then be started from mid-March in the south but should finish correspondingly early or the plants will suffer.

Suggested varieties

Connover's Colossal. A variety with large pointed buds and a general favourite.
Kidner's Pedigree. Produces a large bud and is useful for exhibition.

Celery. Here is a crop that will not respond to any half-hearted or haphazard measures and demands plenty of organic matter and, being a ditch plant, more moisture than many other plants. Although moisture is essential a badly-drained site where water-logging may occur will be more harmful than a little dryness, and time spent digging deep trenches on a very heavy soil may prove a sheer waste of time in a district with a high rainfall. In this case it would be better to dig in plenty of manure and plant on the flat instead of excavating.

Where the soil is a foot or more in depth, well drained, and in good heart from years of cultivating, a trench approximately 16 in. in depth should be taken out. The bottom of the trench should be forked through and manured. The trench bottom should be spread with a thick layer of manure if you can get it or otherwise put in plenty of well-rotted compost. A layer 5 or 6 in. deep will not be too much and this should be firmed. Over this place a 4- or 5-in. layer of good top spit soil. If double rows are to be planted the trench should be 18 in. wide but for a single row 15 in. will be ample. The excavated soil should be placed along each side of the trench in the form of low mounds and on these various catch crops such as lettuce, dwarf beans, radish etc. can be grown. The reason for growing in a trench is not that the plants need such deep planting but to facilitate blanching later on.

Three types of celery are available: white, pink and red; and there are also dwarf varieties. The white varieties are rather tender and easily damaged by frost, while the pink and red varieties are hardier. The white should always be used first and grown for early work. You do need, therefore, to know if the seed you are buying is white or red and whether dwarf or tall. Unless you need the tall kinds for exhibition purposes you will find a so-called dwarf variety is a good type for eating and less trouble.

The main crop is sown in mild heat in the greenhouse about mid-March. Sow in a seed tray filled with a light compost that has been watered a few hours previous to sowing. After sowing cover by sifting a little fine

compost over the seeds and press down with
a presser to ensure good contact with soil
and seed. Celery seeds germinate freely so be
sure to sow sparsely. Cover the box with
glass and brown paper and as soon as
germination has been effected remove the
glass and paper and put the box on a shelf
near the light. As soon as the seedlings can
be handled they sould be pricked off into
further boxes using a rather stronger compost. Prick out at 3 in. apart. Water via a
fine rose. Sowings made in mid-February
will provide an early crop and the latest crop
will need to be sown in early April. Sowings
made too early are liable to bolt.

In late May or early June after being
hardened off the young plants can be set out
in their permanent quarters. The plants
should then be about 4 in. high and a spacing
of 9–10 in. given for a single row. Allow 12
in. between the plants for a double row.
Plant out after a shower if you can but if the
weather is dry give a good watering after
planting. Do not stagger the plants in a
double row as this will make earthing-up

more difficult. Keep the trench free from
weed growth by careful hoeing and do not
allow the plants to become dry at any time.
During the summer give an occasional spray
with clear water and remove any basal
growths that appear.

Celery must be blanched before it can be
eaten and this is done by earthing up at
regular intervals. A preliminary earthing-up
is done by bringing soil up loosely round the
base of the plants and half way up the stems.
This will allow for expansion. The first real
earthing up is done when the plants are
about 12 in. high. This will be about mid-
August. When earthing-up grasp the plant
firmly with one hand and bring the loose
soil up round the plant. Do not bring the soil
quite up to the leaves. Another earthing-up
is done in three weeks' time and the final
earthing up-in October when the soil should
be brought up to the top of the stems, leaving
the leaves above. Before the last earthing-up
place a tie of raffia round the plant just
under the leaves. Finish off the earthing-up
by forming steep sides to the ridges and

Loosening up the soil preparatory to earthing up celery.

Rhubarb is easily forced into growth by covering the
stools with barrels in December.

firming and smoothing with the spade. Throughout the earthing-up process take care to use fine soil and avoid getting crumbs into the heart of the plant.

An alternative to earthing-up (and much less trouble) is to use a cardboard tube or a land drain. Some growers wrap the plants with brown paper. Wide rubber bands make good ties and can be slipped up the plants as required.

There is a self-blanching celery which, if well grown, gives good results and can be ready in August. This needs no earthing-up but to assist blanching the plants are set as close as 6 in. apart. If seed is sown in February in heat and the plants set out in a frame in April, sticks can be had during July. The light can come off the frame in early May.

Suggested varieties

Sandringham Dwarf. A white variety (early).

Clayworth Prize. Pink.

Standard Bearer. Red, rather larger and late.

Golden Self-blanching. Very early and needs no blanching. Will not stand the winter.

Rhubarb. This often neglected plant is worth more than the unfair treatment it so often receives. Yet it can be a most useful crop to have at hand in the early spring. It is by no means difficult to grow and equally easy to forward in the early days of spring.

To grow good rhubarb the site should be deeply dug and manured. The crowns should be set at 3 ft. apart. The site should be an open one and not under a tree or in any old corner that is not considered good enough to grow anything else.

The quickest way to establish a bed is to plant crowns in November or March. Take out a hole on the prepared site big enough to take the roots without cramping them. See that fine soil is pushed down between the roots and the whole plant made firm with the buds just below the surface of the soil.

The mistake so many make is to start pulling before the plants have had a chance to build themselves up. Do not pull any sticks until the plants have been in the ground for a year. Usually rhubarb is over-pulled and underfed. If you want plenty of nice tender sticks the plant must have a chance to build itself up, and the rule should be never to pull until all the leaves have gone, and to limit the pulling season to three months. If you plant several roots you will be able to take a few sticks from each.

You can lift and divide the crowns every three or four years. Dig right round the plant to facilitate lifting. It is better to renew the stock in this way by planting up just two or three new crowns every year or two than hanging on to the old and exhausted stools.

Early supplies can easily be had from the open garden by covering one or two crowns in December with a low skeleton framework and covering it with manure and leaves or simply inverting a large pot or barrel over the stools. If you have a greenhouse you can dig up two or three roots in November and leave them out in all weathers until needed. The crowns should then be placed under the greenhouse staging and kept dark. A temperature of 7°C. (45°F.) will produce early sticks. Keep the crowns moist and syringe over the sticks with tepid water now and then, but no not expose to more light than you can help or the colour will be spoiled.

Varieties

The Sutton. A good maincrop variety.

Prince Albert. A tender variety. Early.

Champagne. For forcing and early pulling outside.

Spinach. This is one of the most health-giving vegetables we have and many people like to have a supply at hand right through the year. There are others who do not like its taste. Whether we like it or not there are two kinds—the round or summer spinach and the prickly spinach. Prickly is a little hardier and less likely to run to seed but the main difference is in the seed itself, one is round-seeded and the other prickly and a nuisance to sow.

Good rich soil is necessary if you want tender spinach and when grown on soil that is retentive of moisture it will grow quickly and be far less liable to bolt, than when grown on indifferent soil and allowed to become dry. During the summer it appreciates some shade and is quite happy between rows of peas or beans.

The first sowing of round spinach can be made during March and successive sowings should be made until July. Sow in drills 12 in. apart and 1 in. deep and thin to 6 in. apart as soon as the seedlings can be handled. On soils that are inclined to dry out and become hot, the drills during the summer can be made in shallow trenches. This will enable water to be given more easily. Where successive sowings are to be made thoughout the summer a sowing should be made every fortnight to maintain the succession.

If a generous sowing is made a few of the larger leaves can be picked from a number of plants rather than denuding some plants of all their leaves.

Winter or prickly spinach is sown from July onwards. It is sown in the same way as the round spinach and needs the same treatment.

If cloches can be spared a crop can be had throughout the winter and in addition to the protection gained the leaves will be unspoiled by mud splashes. Sowings made in September and November, if cloched before the harder weather sets in, will provide pickings throughout the winter and a further sowing under cloches made in February will carry on the supply. Again generous sowings should be made so that the plants can be picked over again and again.

There are several substitutes for spinach. There is spinach beet, sometimes listed as perpetual beet, which produces a continuous supply of large leaves Sowings are made during April and again in August. The rows should be 15 in. apart and the plants thinned to 9 in. Gather the leaves regularly

Forced seakale. The clusters of forced growth are taken by cutting the 'thong' an inch below the leaves. Photo: Messrs Sutton & Sons Ltd.

as soon as they are large enough, even if you cannot use them. This will encourage further leaf growth.

Seakale spinach forms another substitute. The leaves are eaten as spinach and the broad stalk and mid-rib is used as seakle. It is grown in the same way as spinach beet. The leaves are large, thick and silvery white in colour.

Varieties

Goliath. A round-seed summer spinach.

Long Standing Prickly. The prickly or winter spinach.

Seakale. This delicious vegetable is not nearly so well known as it deserves to be. It will grow on almost any soil so long as it is well dug and fertile. The roots or 'thongs' are planted in March and should be set 2 ft. apart. Seed is also sown in March, thinned out to 6 in. and transplanted the next spring to its permanent quarters. It is better to buy or beg thongs for planting as it will be nearly two years before the blanched shoots can be produced from seed.

Water and feed regularly during the growing season, and in autumn after the leaves have died down fork over the ground. In November cover the roots with large pots or boxes and heap over with manure or leaves or a mixture of both. Special pots were once obtainable for this job. Covering the roots will forward and blanch the young growth. The blanched growth is cut when the shoots are some 7 or 8 in. long. It will take seven or eight weeks to force under pots or boxes outdoors.

The crop can be forced indoors but it only needs a temperature of 7°–10°C. (45°– 50°F.). Too high a temperature will result in thin wiry shoots. Seakale is forced in much

Fig. 17. Forcing seakale in a large pot. The top pot is stood on the bottom one to exclude light.

the same way as rhubarb and must have complete darkness. Lift the roots when the leaves wither and trim off the side growths, leaving the tap root. The pencil-like long roots cut off should be shortened to 6 in. and stored in sand or dry earth for planting out in the spring. If, when trimming, a straight cut is made across the top and a slanting cut at the bottom there will be no difficulty in planting them the right way up when the time comes. Choose the thickest and straightest for replanting.

The roots are placed in pots or boxes for forcing. Set the roots 4 in. apart in the boxes; a 9-in. pot will hold six thongs. A good place to stand the roots is under the greenhouse staging. Another box or pot of similar size inverted over the first will ensure darkness. Pack soil and peat between the roots and keep it nicely moist. The bunch of shoots that will appear on each root will be ready to cut in about five weeks. The whole bunch of shoots is taken by cutting off the top $\frac{1}{2}$ in. of the thong. (*Fig. 17.*)

10 *The Cabbage Family*

The cabbage family forms a group of well-known vegetables and few gardens large or small will be found without a few 'greens'. They all need a well worked and consolidated soil that has been generously treated with organic material and has a sufficiency of lime.

In general the seed is sown on a seed bed, the seedlings pricked out into a nursery bed and finally planted out in their permanent quarters. In some cases the pricking out into a nursery bed is omitted. The seed in this case must be very sparsely sown, the seedlings thinned as necessary and later transferred to their final quarters. When time allows, pricking out makes for a better root system and more sturdy plants that, when finally transplanted, suffer less check. You can, of course, buy plants from a nursery or shop but it is far more satisfying to raise your own.

A seed bed 6 ft. × 4 ft. will be large enough to produce all the plants needed for the average garden. If only a few plants are wanted the seed can be sown on a small area between other crops. But in the main where several varieties and types may be required a proper seed bed will be neccessary. It is important that this should be well cultivated for the idea that a seed bed can be any old useless corner is quite wrong and a good clean start will make for a successful finish. The soil should be well dug over and in good heart but you don't need a lot of fresh manure. Work into the top few inches old sifted compost and a good dressing of moistened peat together with a 2 oz. to the square yard dressing of superphosphate. Previous to sowing, dust over the surface with hydrated lime. The seed is easy to sow and should be sown in shallow drills $\frac{1}{2}-\frac{3}{4}$ in. deep depending on the nature of the soil.

When about to transplant do not just yank the plants out from the bed by carelessly pulling. It is advisable to water the bed some hours previously and loosen the plants with a fork. This will ensure a plant that is turgid and one which will suffer little root damage. Such a plant will soon recover and suffer little check. Plant firmly; not by jabbing at the root with a dibber but by pressing the soil round the plant by lightly treading, particularly on the lighter soils.

Using a wise selection of seed varieties a continuous supply of greenstuff can be had throughout the year. This will not be achieved by one large sowing but by several. As with other crops, unless relatively small sowings are made there will be a superabundance at one time and an acute shortage at another. There is a wide choice of types and varieties to grow ranging from Brussels sprouts and cauliflowers to the humble kales. These kales should not be despised for they will still be available when a hard winter has held up other greenstuff.

Cabbage. There is a wide variety of cabbage available including cabbages to mature in the spring, during the summer and in the autumn, the crinkled leaf type (Savoys), coleworts and the red cabbage for pickling. Some are ball-shaped and some conical or pointed. There are large cabbages and small almost ball-like cabbages. It will be realized that a continuity of supply can be arranged by sowing appropriate varieties.

First then, there is what is known as spring cabbage. This is a crop that is eagerly anticipated by many people and therefore a crop that should not be missed. The seeds are sown in July or August. It is usual to sow in July in the north and either late July or mid-August in the south. This sowing should

'Ellam's Dwarf Early'. A popular and beautifully shaped cabbage for autumn sowing and early spring cutting. Photo: Messrs W. J. Unwin Ltd.

Cabbage, 'Flower of Spring'. A large solid cabbage that is not quite so early as some but produces large hearts that stand firm over a long period. Photo: Messrs Sutton & Sons Ltd.

provide heads from March or April. But it is essential to sow the right kind. These are listed as being for autumn sowing and will not necessarily be suitable for sowing at other times.

The normal procedure for sowing is carried out and the plants should be put out during late September or early October. They can follow the early potatoes, peas etc. and as the ground would have been well manured for these crops it will be just right for the spring cabbage. There is no need to dig this ground deeply, but a dressing of hydrated lime should be given at the rate of 6 oz. per square yard if the soil is at all acid. Space the plants at 15–18 in. apart with 2 ft. between the rows.

Keep the rows free from weeds by hoeing when the ground is workable and if the garden is in an exposed position draw up some soil round the base of the plants. Always re-firm any plants that may be lifted

by frost or blown about by strong winds. A side-dressing of nitrate of soda should be given in late February and repeated in March. This should be at the rate of 1 oz. per yard run.

After cutting the heads remove the old stalks if the site is needed right away for another crop, but if the stumps are left for a few weeks and the basal leaves left on, a useful crop of young greens will be had from them.

Close planting in the rows is sometimes done in the autumn. If the plants are set out at 7–9 in. apart it will be possible in the very early days of spring to cut and use alternate plants as spring greens, leaving the remainder to mature as fully grown cabbage.

Varieties suggested for this sowing: *Early Market*. A useful smallish cabbage for early cutting. *Durham Early*. A somewhat larger cabbage; early and a great favourite especially in the north as it is hardier than

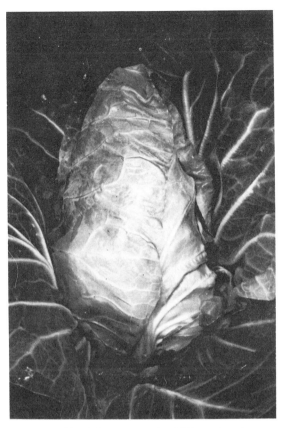

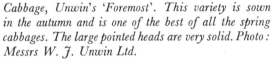

Cabbage, Unwin's 'Foremost'. This variety is sown in the autumn and is one of the best of all the spring cabbages. The large pointed heads are very solid. Photo: Messrs W. J. Unwin Ltd.

Cabbage, 'Primo'. A ball-headed variety that is very compact and dwarf in habit. Usually sown in March for cutting in July. Photo: Messrs W. J. Unwin Ltd.

some. *Ellams Dwarf Early.* Another well-known variety. It is of dwarf habit with a beautifully shaped pointed heart and very suitable for a small garden.

Summer and autumn cabbage. In early February a sowing made under cloches or in the frame will provide plants for setting out in April and will provide heads that will quickly follow after the autumn-sown varieties. A further sowing can be made in the open in mid-March and the varieties suggested will mature quickly. The ground for these spring sowings can be enriched with manure or good compost plus a dressing of general fertilizer at the rate of 3 oz. per square yard. Sowings made during April and May of one of the more slowly maturing varieties will provide heads in the late autumn and well into the winter.

Varieties for the spring sowings can be:

Greyhound. An early variety of conical shape and a great favourite. *Velocity.* A round cabbage of the Primo type. Both of these are particularly suitable for the February and March sowings. *Golden Acre* is another quick-maturing kind with solid medium-shaped heads. *January King* is probably the latest maturing variety. It is very hardy and often stands until April. It has a touch of purple on the outer leaves. *Christmas Drumhead.* Of compact habit it can be planted a little closer than other maincrop cabbages. These are sown in late April and planted out during May or in early June. They should be given rather more generous spacing than the earlier kinds and the rows should be 2 ft. apart.

Savoys. The Savoy cabbage is a hardier form of cabbage and suited for standing through the winter. It is grown in exactly the same way as other cabbages, the seed being sown in April.

Varieties: *Winter King.* Very dark green. Ready to cut in November and December. *Ormskirk Late Green.* A popular late variety that will stand into February and March. Sow late in April.

Red cabbage. This is of the drumhead type. It is usual to sow the red pickling cabbage in early spring but it can also be sown in the late summer and over-wintered with a little protection. Planted out the next spring very large heads will be ready in the autumn. From spring sowings the heads are smaller but usually plenty large enough. Grow as you would cabbages. *Early Blood Red* is a good variety that has medium-sized heads but very solid and the colour is good.

Brussels sprouts. In considering this very popular vegetable several essential points must be borne in mind. First, a good strain of seed is necessary, bearing in mind that there are early and late varieties and that some are dwarf and others tall. In a small garden the more dwarf kinds will be best. It must also be remembered that brussels must be grown on fertile and well-consolidated ground and given liberal spacing. A well-grown brussels plant will provide you with good firm sprouts from bottom to top, closely and evenly spaced and without any tendency to 'blow' or open.

The necessity to plant on well-consolidated soil cannot be overstressed if firm sprouts are to be produced without 'blowers'. The ground should be dug and manured well in advance of the planting date. Leave the soil rough for the weather to break down and give a dressing of lime over the surface. If no lime has been given for some time a dressing of 6 oz. to the square yard of hydrated lime will not be too much. On the light soils digging and manuring can be left until a little later. In the spring when the ground can be worked the surface should be broken down and levelled and a few days before planting dressed with a complete fertilizer which should be worked into the top 2 or

A basket of well-grown sprouts. Photo: Messrs Sutton & Sons Ltd.

A good stand of Brussels sprouts. The variety is 'Triple X'. Photo: Messrs J. Harrison.

Good keeping onions can be grown from 'sets'. The tiny sets should be planted during March.
Photo: Dobies.

Salad onions. 'White Lisbon' is the best variety to grow.
Photo: Suttons.

(Lower right) Leeks 'The Lyon'. A well grown specimen of this favourite variety.
Photo: Dobies.

Radishes. A favourite variety for early work—'Crimson Globe'.
Photo: Suttons.

The lettuce 'Buttercrunch' will provide a delicious base for a salad.
Photo: Thompson and Morgan

3 in. A dressing of 3 oz. per square yard can be given. If manuring was on the meagre side this can be increased to 4 oz.

For an early crop the seeds are sown in the frame or under a cloche or two in late January or February. The seedlings must be hardened off before planting out during April. Normal sowings are made during March or early April and should be planted out during May.

Choose if you can a showery day to plant out or be prepared to water the plants if the soil is dry. A spacing of 2 ft. 6 in. between the plants and 2 ft. 6 in. between the rows will not be too generous. Take care to firm the earth well around the plants. Where tall and late varieties are grown, if rows are planted 3 ft. apart this is advantageous.

Regular hoeing to keep down weed growth should be undertaken and two or three light side-dressings of a complete fertilizer given during the growing season. Leaves that have become old and yellow should be removed from the base of the plants by bending them upwards and snapping them off. On no account remove the heads of the plants; they will help to protect the sprouts. They can be cut out and used as greens when most of the sprouts have been gathered. Gather the sprouts from the bottom upwards taking a few from each plant (*Fig. 18*).

Varieties suggested: *Thor* F₁ hybrid). Early and can be picked in September. Small round sprouts of medium size. *Irish Elegance*. A maincrop variety giving high yields of excellent sprouts. Medium height. *Cambridge No. 5*. A splendid late variety. Tall and bearing sprouts of regular size and shape. *The Wroxton*. An old variety and popular in the north. Medium height producing sprouts in mid season. Very suitable for the smaller gardens.

Cauliflowers and broccoli. Both cauliflowers and broccoli are botanically the same but the cauliflower differs from the broccoli in that it is less hardy and therefore grown during the spring and summer. Broccoli can be had during the winter and early spring.

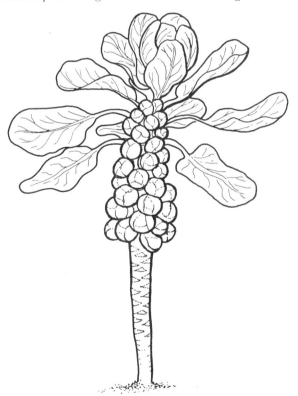

Fig. 18. Brussel sprouts must be gathered from the base of the stem upwards.

The cauliflower is considered to be of finer texture and of better flavour than the broccoli. It is said to be the queen of vegetables and needs more care and fussing over than any other vegetable and is more particular as to growing conditions than most. I remember an old gardener once reminding me that to grow cauliflowers one needs muck, muscle and moisture. How right he was! Unless you are prepared to dig deeply, manure heavily and be generous with water it would be better to leave the summer cauliflower alone and rely on the more hardy and less choosy broccoli. But both are gross feeders.

Seeds for the earliest crops are sown in the autumn and over-wintered in the frame. The seedlings should be grown as hardily as possible and ventilation should be given whenever weather permits. During hard weather sacks or mats should be laid over the light to keep off frost.

The soil in the frame should not be rich but rather on the poor side and old potting soil would do nicely with a sprinkling of superphosphate and some peat, plus a dusting of lime. The seedlings are often potted up separately in 3-in. pots and plunged up to the rims in ashes in the frame. This does entail more work but it produces fine plants which can be planted out without a check of any sort. In either case the plants must be hardened off before being planted out in April 15 in. apart with 18 in. between the rows. An early sowing is often made under cloches or in the frame in late January or early February in the south and west for an early cut, but the normal sowing is made in March or early April. These will not of course produce such early heads but they are far less trouble.

The plants from this sowing must be given a little more space if the variety is of a larger type and 18 in. between plants and 2 ft. between the rows will be needed. Take care when planting to discard any 'blind' plants,

A well-grown cauliflower seedling ready to plant out.

i.e. those without a growing centre, as these will not produce a head. Always plant cauliflowers with a trowel and do not plant too deeply. This may sometimes induce blindness. Plant with as little root disturbance as possible and water in the plant if the soil is at all dry.

The site for cauliflowers should be dug and manured well ahead of planting to ensure consolidation and good heads. You cannot overdo the manure and a complete fertilizer should be lightly worked in before planting. Fish manure at the rate of 4 oz. per square yard will make a good dressing.

During the growing season keep the plants free from weeds and give an occasional feed of liquid manure and soot water. These can be given alternately. As the curds form snap a leaf over to protect them from bright sun. Cauliflowers are never happy in hot dry weather especially if they are growing on a very light soil.

Suggested varieties for early and summer crops: *Sutton's Polaris*. A favourite early cauliflower producing first-class heads in early June from an autumn sowing. *Forerunner*. Suitable for early sowing. An excellent variety also for sowing in March. *All the Year Round*. Can be sown at any time and appropriately named, producing large white heads that mature according to the time of sowing.

Broccoli. In general terms broccoli needs much the same treatment as cauliflowers but there will be no question of early sowing as the plants will produce heads in the autumn and through the winter if long-standing varieties are included. They need a longer season of growth than cauliflowers. The rule in obtaining a succession (if you

Bending cauliflower leaves over the curd to protect it from strong sunshine.

Cauliflower, 'Polaris'. A new variety that is early and probably the largest-headed of the early-heading varieties. It produces pure white curds. Photo: Messrs Sutton & Sons Ltd.

have room for them) is to sow the earliest varieties first and follow with the late ones, taking care to plant out in the same order. The soil must have been deeply dug and well manured but be firm and well settled before planting.

Broccoli is sown in April for use from November until January or February and from late April into May for heading from February until May the next year.

Here are some suggested varieties that will give you heads when the summer cauli-flowers have finished.

Variety		Sow	Cut
Majestic	The last of the summer cauliflowers. Produces a large head.	E. Apr.	Sept.–Oct.
Veitch's Self-Pro-tecting	A reliable variety heading from Nov.	M. Apr.	Nov.–Dec.
Snow's Winter White	A valuable mid-winter variety.	L. Apr.	Dec.. Jan
Mammoth Spring White (Carter's)	Large and beautifully white heads.	L. Apr.	Jan.–Mar.–
Leamington	A reliable and popular variety.	May	Mar.–Apr.
Thanet (Sutton's)	Less affected by frost than most other varie-ties and useful for the north and very exposed districts.	L. May	Apr.–May
St. George	Large snow-white heads of good quality.	L. May	Apr.–Jun.

Sprouting broccoli. This is a first-class winter crop and an excellent standby when other greens are in short supply. They produce masses of small heads over a long period and can be cut as required. *Early Purple Sprouting* is sown in March for cutting in December and January. The shoots are cut when they are from 9 to 12 in. long. There is also a *Late Purple Sprouting*. This should be sown in April and will be in cut from February to March or even April.

White sprouting broccoli is sown in April. It is not so hardy as the purple and is better suited to the more sheltered gardens. It will be available at the same time as the late purple.

There is also a green sprouting broccoli sometimes known as Italian or calabresse. It should be sown in March. The plants bear a large central head in the late summer and after this has been cut shoots grow from each leaf joint and bear a small curd on the top with a few leaves round and under the curd. The shoots are produced over a long period and make very good eating.

All of these plants make plenty of growth and need generous spacing.

Kale or borecole. The various kales are generally known as 'greens' and make a most useful contribution to the supply of fresh greenstuff during the winter and spring. They are available at times when all other greenstuff has been brought to a standstill by a very hard winter and it is just as well to keep a few kales in reserve in case other greenstuff becomes scarce. They all produce a large crop of side shoots over a long period.

Kales are sown in April on a seed bed and planted out during June. Like all the cabbage family they do best on a firm and well-cultivated soil but they are not so exacting in their demands as other members of the family. The plants should be given a spacing of 2 ft. each way. Here are the more popular kales grown:

Curly or Scotch kale. This has tightly curled and crested foliage. It is extremely hardy.

Asparagus kale. Produces succulent young shoots in the early spring as soon as the harder weather is over. Thin long shoots.

Thousand-headed kale. This yields an im-mense crop of side shoots early in the year and will continue to do so until the late spring.

Cottager's kale. Almost as hardy as curly kale but is somewhat coarse and less pleasant to eat. It needs rather more space than others.

11 *Bulb crops*

Onions. Onions seem to have been cultivated long before recorded history and the Israelites in their wanderings complained to Moses about the lack of onions, leeks and garlic, which they had been accustomed to eat in Egypt.

A great deal has been written about the preparation of the ground for onions, so that the beginner gets the impression that only the expert is likely to produce a good crop. This may well be so when bulbs of 4 or 5 lb. are to be produced, but the housewife prefers a much smaller onion for cooking.

Onions do, nevertheless, require careful growing, a deep fertile soil and ground that has been well cultivated for some years. When preparing the bed double-digging should be practised and dung or good compost incorporated with the bottom as well as the top spit. This should be done in autumn for it is important that sowing or planting should be done on soil that is consolidated, especially on the lighter soils. This does not mean that the soil should be rolled or trodden down like concrete, and any firming should have regard to the nature of the soil. A well-prepared bed that is retentive of moisture but well drained may serve for many years, and it is well worth while taking some extra trouble in preparing

Onion, 'The Sutton Globe'. A long-keeping globe-shaped variety. It is a heavy cropper and ripens early. Photo: Messrs Sutton & Sons Ltd.

The thorough harvesting of the onion crop can be helped by covering with cloches both before and after lifting.

Onion, 'Reliance'. A flattish-shaped onion of mild flavour and a wonderful keeper. Best results follow an autumn sowing but it will also succeed from a March sowing. Photo: Messrs W. J. Unwin Ltd.

such a bed. The addition of gritty material, rotted straw, etc. will assist drainage on a heavy soil and lots of peat and composted material will be an advantage on a lighter soil.

When preparing the bed in subsequent years there will be no need to double-dig unless water-logging takes place but each year dig in a good barrow-load of manure or compost to 6 square yards and before planting or sowing give a 4 oz. per square yard dressing of some complete fertilizer with a high potash content, together with any bonfire ash you may have. Also give a light dressing of hydrated lime.

Seed may be sown in the early autumn outdoors, during January in the greenhouse and outdoors in March as soon as the ground is workable. The autumn sowing is made in late August but in the north in early August. In the spring the young plants are thinned out to stand at 6 in. apart, using any thinnings as spring onions, or they can be transplanted to fill any gaps. Good bulbs will be ready during the summer.

The January sowings should be made in boxes in the heated greenhouse. This sowing will produce the large onions seen on the show bench in the autumn. The box should be filled with a light seed compost and well firmed. Sow the seed at approximately ¾ in. apart and only lightly cover, pressing the surface down to ensure contact with soil and seed. After watering with a fine rose place a piece of glass and brown paper over the box. As soon as the seed is through take off the cover and place the box on a shelf near the greenhouse windows. Prick out the seedlings into another box of good potting compost and place the seedlings at approximately 1½ in. apart. In March it will be possible to place the box in a cold frame to harden off preparatory to planting out on the prepared bed in the open. In the more sheltered districts this sowing can be made in the cold frame or under cloches in late January or early February.

Towards the end of March or early April the main spring sowing is made. This will form the main crop for storing through the winter. Sow in shallow drills 12 in. apart and drop the seed thinly along the drills. One is advised to sow onions when the wind is blowing. What is really meant is that the top inch of soil should be almost dry and the bed can be lightly trodden and the drills taken out. Such a condition is ideal for sowing. After covering the seed tamp down along the drills with the rake.

When planting out the January-sown plants (usually during April) choose a showery period and remove the seedlings with as little root disturbance as possible. For really large onions the rows can be 15 in. apart and the plants set at 9 in. in the rows. Always plant with a trowel, making a hole deep enough for the roots to go straight down. Do not plant too deeply. Ideally the plate at the base of the little immature bulb should be almost on top of the soil. Firm planting is necessary.

As soon as the spring-sown seedlings are of any size hoeing should start along the rows and an initial thinning should be done. Aim at leaving the plants to stand eventually at 6 in. apart. Although onions will not tolerate a water-logged condition they need plenty of moisture and the growing crop should never be left to dry out. Also the bulb should form above the ground and when hoeing the tendency must be to draw the soil away from the base of the bulb, taking great care not to nick the bulbs with the hoe.

Onions should ripen naturally but thorough ripening is essential if the crop is to store well. Maturity is indicated when the leaves drop over just above the neck. As the leaves wither the neck shrinks and becomes closed. A bulb with a thick and open neck will not store. Little benefit is had by bending over the tops. If the crop is nicely ripening the leaves will fall over on their own and even if thick-necked bulbs are bent over they will not make good onions for storing. Any such bulbs should be used first. Damage is frequently caused by bending over the leaves. Before attempting to lift the bulbs loosen them with a fork. After lifting lay them to dry in the sun for a time. A good plan is to cover the bulbs with cloches for a time before and after lifting to ensure thorough ripening and drying.

Store by roping the onions and hanging them up in cool and dry quarters or lay them out in slatted trays.

The onion fly is the most serious of pests to be looked for. Parsley sown here and there between the plants is said to keep away the fly. Whizzed naphthalene dusted along the rows is probably better and should always be used after thinning the plants. See also page 103.

Onion sets. Good onions can be grown from what are known as onion 'sets'. These are very small immature onions whose development has been arrested. When planted out in the spring they will complete their growth. Reliable sets can be had from all seedsmen.

The sets are planted during March in the same way as shallots but they should be pushed will into the ground so that they can be covered with an inch of soil. Prepare the site as previously described and cultivate in the normal way.

Where sometimes it is difficult to grow onions from seed, sets are recommended and the onion fly will not attack them.

Spring or salad onions are dealt with under salad crops in Chapter 13.

Suggested varieties

Reliance. Mild flavour and flattish in shape. A good keeper.

Bedfordshire Champion. Globe-shaped and suitable for spring sowing. A well-tried variety and a great favourite.

Autumn Queen. A grand variety for August sowing.

The Queen. A small silver-skinned onion suitable for pickling.

Shallots. Although the old saying that shallots should be planted on the shortest day and harvested on the longest still persists we seldom get round to doing so. As the shallot is one of the hardiest of vegetables it is an advantage if the ground is ready and workable to plant out as early as possible but even when left until March a good crop is often produced, but harvesting will, of course, be late.

If the shallots are planted next to the onions the onion bed, when in the making, can be extended to include shallots, since both need similar soil conditions.

Before planting loosen up the top 2 or 3 in. of soil and press the bulbs into the soil so that only the merest tip is showing and after planting firm the soil round the shoulders of the bulbs to prevent the roots pushing them up. If this happens see that they are re-firmed. The rows should be 12 in. apart and the bulbs spaced at 6 in. in the rows. Where birds are a nuisance some protection in the shape of netting or pea guards is advisable.

Keep the hoe going during growth and, as the crop nears maturity, draw the soil away from the bulbs rather than towards them as with onions. The bulbs should sit on the surface of the soil where they get the benefit of air and sun.

Shallots are usually ready to harvest in July or early August and should be dried in the sun and stored in a cool and dry place.
Varieties

Dutch or Jersey. These form large and almost round bulbs.

The True Red or Yellow: Smaller bulbs for pickling.

Leeks. Given a well-prepared and fertile soil a good crop of leeks can be had with little trouble. The cooler climate of the north is ideally suited to the growing of leeks, where it is a favourite dish. Great rivalry and a variety of methods is encountered in producing the mammoth specimens seen at shows in the north. For the average household where the main effort is directed to produce a good crop of not too large leeks suitable for the kitchen there is no need to go to any great trouble to produce a very satisfying crop.

For exhibition the seed is sown in heat in January and pricked out 1 in. apart. When the seedlings are beginning to grow nicely they should be potted into 3-in. pots filled with a good potting compost such as the John Innes Compost No. 2, when they can be grown on without check in transplanting. The seedlings must be hardened off in March or April ready to go out on a prepared bed at the end of April or early May.

The main sowing is made in March or early April on a prepared seed bed. If the

Well-grown leeks. The variety is 'Improved Musselburgh'. Photo: Messrs Sutton & Sons Ltd.

seed is sparsely sown no thinning should be necessary and when the plants are 5 or 6 in. high they are planted out on the prepared site in rows 12–15 in. apart and 6 in. between the plants. This should be done early in June.

The usual method of planting out the main crop is to draw deep drills as for potatoes and plant along the bottom of the drill. Make a hole some 5 in. deep with a dibber and just drop the plants in so that the leaves are just showing. Do not close the hole; the first rain will carry some soil down. As the leeks grow the drill should be gradually drawn in. If further blanching is necessary earth can be drawn up round the plants in the same way that potatoes are earthed up.

Leeks form an excellent winter vegetable and are most useful from December onwards when the choice of vegetables is reduced, and there seems little point in using them at an early date when so many other vegetables can be had.

Leeks are among the hardiest of vegetables and can be left in the ground throughout the winter and lifted as needed. If very hard frost threatens, however, it is as well to lift a few and heel them in where they can easily be had if the ground is frost-bound.

Suggested varieties

The Lyon. Solid thick stems with dark leaves. An old and reliable variety.

Selected Musselburgh. One of the finest varieties for general use. Popular in the north.

Garlic. Of all the onion family, garlic is the most pungent in flavour and is a favourite condiment and flavouring in Europe. Because of its pungency it is seldom grown in this country, although large quantities are used in the manufacture of pickles and sauces.

Garlic is hardy and can be grown quite well even in colder conditions but it does need a hot and sunny period as it matures and succeeds better in the more southern districts where good ripening is more certain. The cloves are enclosed in a tough sheath and on breaking this open some 10 or more cloves are revealed. These, except for the two or three centre ones, are planted separately 1½–2 in. deep and spaced at 6 in.

apart. The rows (if you plant so many) should be 12 in. apart, but the cloves from one bulb will probably be all that are needed. (*Fig. 19.*)

A good fertile soil is needed and the top 2 in. should be worked down to a fine tilth. If the cloves are planted towards the end of February the ripened bulbs should be ready during August when the foliage will have died down. Loosen the bulbs with a fork and take great care in lifting not to break open the sheath. Store under dry and cool conditions after cleaning off any soil, and thoroughly drying in the sun.

Ripening can be greatly assisted by covering with a few cloches in July and the use of cloches for a month when first planted will enhance the chance of success by giving the plants a flying start.

Variety suggested: Best Italian.

There are several types of onions that differ in some respects from those more usually grown but each has the distinctive flavour common to all the onion tribe. They are generally planted in small groups or clumps and like the better-known types they prefer a well-cultivated and fertile soil.

The potato onion. This is sometimes known as the underground onion and is grown in a similar way to shallots but the bulb should be pressed well into the soil. The bulb when planted will form a cluster of small bulbs of a mild flavour. Planting can be done quite early in the milder parts of the country.

The Welsh onion. Actually this hails from Siberia and is very hardy. The Welsh onion is perhaps better known than the potato onion and plants should be bought in the spring or autumn and planted 3 in. deep. Each plant will produce a bunch of 'spring onions'. The plant is dug up and separated when needed. Clumps can be split up and replanted to maintain a supply. One little plant may well produce some thirty plants.

The tree or Egyptian onion. This must not be planted on the surface but must be placed 3 in. deep and left undisturbed for several years. On the top of the main stem a number of small bulbs will be produced. Bulbs will also form round the old bulb and both are excellent for pickling. The stem should be given some support before the onions on top form.

Chives. These will provide a useful edging to a border as well as being very good in salads or soups where only a mild onion flavour is needed. Close tufts of leaves are formed and if these are regularly cut there will always be a plentiful supply of young and tender material. Old plants can be divided and replanted in the spring 6 in. apart. Seed is sown on a seed bed in March and planted out the following spring.

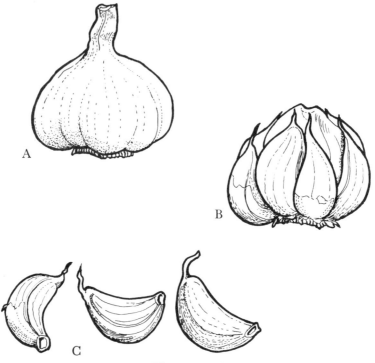

Fig. 19. Garlic.
A. *The bulb covered with sheath.*
B. *The sheath removed showing segments or cloves.*
C. *The cloves which are planted separately.*

12 *Potatoes*

Very few main meals are served in which potatoes in some form or other are not included and every household will use a considerable quantity in the course of a year. In a small garden it is always a question as to whether an area given over to potatoes could be better utilized in growing other crops and many private gardeners will be content to compromise and grow only a few rows of early potatoes and buy in those needed during the rest of the year. On consideration this would seem a wise decision, especially as freshness and flavour will be one of the chief reasons for growing vegetables. While potatoes can be stored quite well without loss of flavour the same cannot be said of peas, lettuce, beans and many, other vegetables.

But if ground is available both early and maincrop potatoes should be grown for it must be remembered that the aim of a farmer or market grower is to grow bulk-producing varieties that look well, store well and travel well. A variety like Golden Wonder, a high-quality potato, will not be found in the shops as it only produces about half the weight of crop of, say, Majestic. And so the grower grows Majestic rather than Golden Wonder—and who can blame him? The private gardener can grow just whichever variety suits his taste. He may like a waxy or solid potato or prefer a floury or mealy one. He can put quality first and will be satisfied with a lighter yield so long as he is getting what he likes.

It would need a whole volume to do justice to the lowly potato, but unfortunately lack of space will permit only a brief guide. Introduced into Europe towards the end of the sixteenth century from South America it is now a staple food in almost every civilized country. The beginner will want to know something of the varieties that can be grown and the reader is advised to study the seed lists sent out by leading seedsmen. For our purpose we can think of them in terms of three classes:

1. Earlies.
2. Second earlies or mid-season.
3. Maincrop.

It is not easy to advise on varieties of potatoes except in general terms. A variety that succeeds in one garden will not necessarily be satisfactory in another. Some have white flesh while others are yellow; some floury or mealy and others waxy and firm. It is better to experiment with several varieties at first and find out which does best on your soil and suits your taste. But always consult the cook. She will also have ideas as to how they cook.

Of the early varieties *Aran Pilot* (white kidney) is very early and a heavy cropper but not particularly well flavoured. *Duke of York* is a yellow flesh variety (kidney) and seems to do well on most soils. It is a favourite as a new potato and is firm when cooked. *Pentland Beauty* is yet another early variety and of more recent introduction. It is oval and creamy in colour and is a heavy cropper.

Mid-season varieties are planted a little later than the earlies and do not mature quite so quickly. *Ulster Chieftan* (sometimes grown as an early variety) is a nice oval and white-fleshed potato. The flavour is said to be best when it is lifted early. *Sharpe's Express* is an old variety that is still popular. Kidney-shaped with pale yellow flesh the tubers are of moderate size and even shape. *Dr. McIntosh* is kidney-shaped with white flesh. Produces tubers of moderate size. Shallow eyes and very suitable for exhibition.

Amongst the many popular maincrop varieties are *Majestic* (sometimes classed as a mid-season variety). It is one of the heaviest of croppers and produced tubers of large size. The quality is good and the tubers kidney-shaped with white flesh. A great favourite, it is best grown on light land that has been well manured. *Catriona.* A well-flavoured good potato that produces huge crops. It does quite well on poorer soils. It is sometimes classed as a mid-season variety. *Golden Wonder.* Probably the best variety introduced. It is kidney-shaped with white flesh. A light cropper but of suberb quality. Stores well. *King Edward VII.* Kidney-shaped and white flesh. The skin is creamy white splashed with red. An old variety that is still popular. Both Golden Wonder and King Edward are good varieties for exhibition.

There are many more varieties to choose from so study your seed lists and be sure to place your order in good time or you may not get the variety you want.

When the seed potatoes arrive they should be placed in boxes or trays to sprout. This is known as chitting and is an essential part of good potato culture. The tubers should be placed in the tray or box with the eye or rose end uppermost. (The rose end is the end with most eyes). If the tray is tilted while you are trying to stand up the potatoes they will not fall over and roll about. Place the trays in a good light and keep frost away. Sprouting potatoes need a temperature of approximately 5°C. (40°F.). They also like an occasional spraying over with tepid water. Sturdy shoots and not too many are wanted. Keep a sharp look-out for greenfly and deal with it straight away. If the seed arrives too late for cutting rub off any long white growths as these are useless. The seed can be cut if necessary but do not rub the cut tuber

A grand crop of potatoes. The variety 'Foremost' is one of the newer varieties and is early and produces a heavy crop of white-skinned oval tubers. Photo: Messrs Sutton & Sons Ltd.

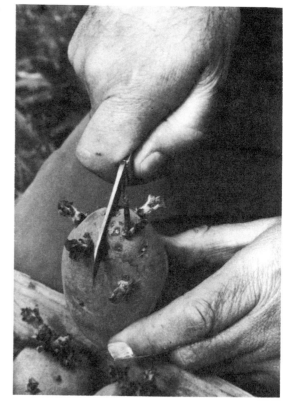

When cutting a tuber make the cut lengthwise and see that each portion has two good sprouts. Do this just before planting.

Sprouted potato sets ready for planting. They should be set in trays on arrival and placed in a good light. A temperature of 40°F. is ideal.

in lime as is sometimes advised. If cutting is done just before planting there is no need to do anything but to keep the cut moist until the set is planted. Cut lengthwise and see that each portion has two good sprouts.

Potatoes will grow on almost any soil but the best crops are produced from a light loamy soil. Digging and manuring should be done before Christmas if possible and the soil left rough for the weather to break down. Farmyard manure should be dug in at the rate of a large barrow-load to 10 square yards but do not lime the ground. Some growers like to put the manure or compost along the bottom of the drill and cover with a few inches of soil. Others like a thick layer of leaf-mould. In this case the drill should be a little deeper. In addition a complete fertilizer should be lightly dusted along each side of the drill before covering in.

For planting the first earlies mid-March is a good guide. The mid-season varieties will need to go in at the end of March or early April. Maincrop varieties can wait until towards the end of April or even early May. The normal distance to plant is:

First earlies—10 to 12 in. apart in rows 1 ft. 9 in. apart.
Mid-season varieties—15 in. apart in rows 2 ft. apart.
Main crop—16 in. apart in rows 2 ft. 6 in. apart.

The tubers should not be deeper than 4 in., and 3 inches will be deep enough for the first earlies.

The drill can be taken out with a spade or a Canterbury hoe which is an excellent tool for taking out the large drills. The tubers should be pushed into the bottom of the drill or into the soil covering a layer of manure. The sprouts should be uppermost and take care not to break off the sprouts as they are very brittle. Never use a dibber to plant potatoes. Before covering in mark both ends of the row with a stick. When the shoots appear, especially in the case of the earlies, they should be protected as far as possible from any frost by pulling a little soil over them or by using a little straw. The lightest of covering will do the trick. Cloches are, of course, ideal when an extra early crop is desired.

When the work for some reason has had to be delayed and time is short the seed is sometimes planted as digging proceeds. While this is not the best method by any means, it does make for quickness, and if this method has to be used always use a line to keep the rows straight and take great care to mark each row.

As the plants grow earthing-up must be done. The object of this is to help keep the plants upright and to prevent the potatoes showing on the surface of the soil where they would become green and useless. Start earthing-up when the plants are some 9 in. high and draw up the soil from either side to about half the height of the haulm. Before doing so hoe along the rows to ensure a fine texture and take the opportunity to dust a light dressing of some complete fertilizer along each side so that it is drawn up with the soil. A further earthing-up will be necessary in a month's time but never leave less than 6 in. of haulm exposed.

Lift the earlies as soon as the new potatoes are big enough to warrant lifting. As new potatoes are a great treat at first they can be lifted when they are about the size of a large walnut or a bantam's egg. You can find out how large they are by grubbing in the soil with your hand and exposing or feeling the tubers with the fingers. The main crop may be left until the tops die down and a root can be lifted to see if the skins have become firm and set. If lifted too soon when the skin is tender the tubers are liable to go soft in store. Lift and handle carefully so that no bruising takes place and lay out in the open to dry for some hours. In some districts slugs may be a nuisance at this time and it may be necessary to lift in good time if the crop is to be saved. Lift with a flat-tined fork by inserting the fork between the plants and lift with a forward motion. If the haulm has not fully died down as may be the case in some seasons, cut it off 6 in. above the ground before lifting, Remember that the drier you get the crop after lifting the better it will keep.

Potatoes can be stored in a clamp or put into boxes or barrels which should be stood in a frost-proof place. They must be well shaded from bright light and the temperature of the store should not exceed 5°–7°C. (40°–45°F.).

A note on potato blight will be found in Chapter 18.

13 *Salads*

Salads would seem to be far less complicated and elaborate than they were many years ago. The head gardener of James II was of the opinion that a salad should consist of at least thirty-five ingredients. One cannot help thinking that what is sometimes served as a salad would be more interesting if a few of those forgotten herbs and roots were used today. Yet, it must be remembered that the vegetables that go to make a salad today have been greatly improved and with some thought and trouble a dish can be presented that is not only a delight to look at but equally nice to eat.

It is not proposed to mention here all the ingredients that may go to make a salad. Turnips, carrots, cucumbers, tomatoes, peas and beans, sweet corn and other vegetables will all add to the dish. These will be found elsewhere in this book and the housewife will know how to deal with them. It is only the principal vegetables that can be mentioned in this chapter.

Lettuce. There are few gardeners who do not grow lettuce for it forms the basic material of most salads. And so, if you have made up your mind to put that piece of land to some useful and profitable purpose you will certainly be bullied into growing a supply of lettuce. Supplies can easily be had from May until October—and if you have a few cloches, from April until November.

We are apt to think of lettuce as either cabbage or cos, forgetting that both fall into several groups, especially the cabbage lettuce, and it is most important to sow the right variety or type for the job. So study your seed lists carefully and do not be tempted to sow in the autumn any seed left over from the spring sowing. If you prefer a lettuce with crisp and crinkled leaves rather than a smooth and soft lettuce you must sow the appropriate variety.

The advice so frequently given to sow just 'a pinch' of seed at one time and at frequent intervals is seldom put into practice with the result that for two or three weeks there is a glut of lettuce which the family cannot cope with and you cannot even give them away. This is followed by a period of famine. Sow just a few seeds every three weeks on any vacant ground or as a catch or inter-crop between other vegetables and you can have a constant supply of young and tender lettuce over many months.

Lettuce thrive on a soil that is well supplied with organic matter. A soil well charged with humus will hold the moisture that the plants must have if they are to grow quickly and prove tender eating. Give a dressing of a complete fertilizer before sowing.

Sowing in the open. Sowings can be made outdoors from early March onwards. A fine surface tilth is needed because the seed is very small, but the underlying soil should be firm. Take out shallow drills with a stick or the corner of the hoe and scatter the seed thinly along the row. Rows should be 12 in. apart and the plants left to stand 9–10 in. apart. Give an initial thinning to single out the plants as soon as they can be handled, otherwise they will quickly become drawn, so never leave the seedlings to crowd one another. Keep the hoe going and do not let the plants suffer from lack of water. Successional sowings can be made until August in accordance with the family needs.

Lettuce seed can also be sown outdoors during August—early August in the more exposed districts and late August in the south. These will over-winter in the open and heart up in the spring. Cutting should be had in

Two rows of cabbage lettuce inter-cropped with cos lettuce can be grown under the·Chase Low barn cloches. Photo: Messrs Expandite Ltd.

May. Seeds can also be sown on a seed bed and planted out in October. In February a side dressing of sulphate of ammonia should be given as a tonic. You must be careful to sow one of the very hardy varieties specially designed for this sowing. It is, however, except in the milder districts, somewhat of a gamble and the lettuce are apt to be on the coarse side.

Frame and cloche cultivation. For the earliest supplies seeds should be sown in mid-October, choosing one of the varieties specially suited to this sowing. Two rows can be sown under most cloches and the plants thinned out to stand eventually at 9 in. apart. Give a thinning out in the early days and leave the final thinning until the turn of the year. If sufficient cloches are not available at the time of sowing then sow on a seed bed and cover with one or two cloches. It is equally important to thin these seedlings

if the sowing proves to be too thick in order to produce sturdy and strong little plants.

The seedlings should be planted out under other cloches or in the frame as soon as they are large enough. Get this done during December. The weather is often mild until Christmas but very uncertain afterwards and sowings may be delayed too long to get a really early cut. Have the light over the frame or the cloches set out over the site a week or ten days previous to planting to warm and dry the top inch or so of soil.

Sowings are also made in the frame or under cloches in late January or early February. Cultivation will be the same as for the autumn-sown lettuce. The cloches or the light can be dispensed with during April and the crop will follow very closely after the autumn-sown lettuce. In the north a similar sowing can be made in a heated frame.

During the winter ventilate whenever

Tomato 'Sleaford Abundance', a new bush variety of tomato. A first rate variety for outdoor work. It grows to a height of 12 in.

Photo: Dobies.

Tomato 'Moneymaker'. A well tried variety. The plants were set out under cloches in April. Decloched in early June. Photo taken late July.

Photo: L.N.F.

(Above)

Tomato 'Alicante'. A modern and early variety of nice size and flavour. Does very well in the open.

Photo: Suttons.

Sweet Corn 'Kelvedon Glory'. An early variety producing good even cobs.

Photo: Unwins.

(Lower left) Sweet Corn 'Golden Bantam'.

Photo: Dobies.

Ridge Cucumber 'Burpee'. This is a new early F_1 variety. The skin is smooth and practically spineless.

Photo: Unwins.

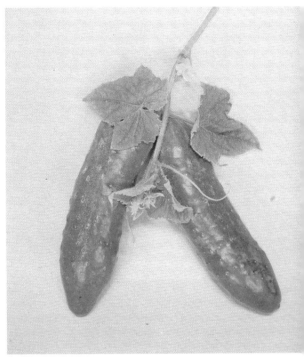

weather conditions permit by raising the light at the back. Do this also on those sunny mornings that so often follow a frost when the rise in temperature under the glass may be too rapid. Where cloches are concerned keep the ends closed. Glass cloches are to some extent self-ventilating or may have means of opening a roof pane. Plastic tunnel cloches can be ventilated by raising the plastic sheeting on one side—the lee side of course. If room allows, lettuce can be grown on either side of peas or beans under cloches or a row of carrots can be sown between rows of lettuce. Spring onions can also be sown between the lettuce rows, thus using all available protected space.

It is most unlikely that watering will be necessary during the winter but in the early spring and especially in the frame, some watering may have to be done. In that case water between the plants and not over them.

Cos lettuce. Mention must be made of the cos lettuce. It is preferred by some because of its crisp and somewhat nutty-flavoured leaves. In general it is grown in the same way as cabbage lettuce but while some varieties are self-folding others will need tying up. Tying up consists of passing raffia around the lettuce when it approaches maturity. The tie should not be too tight so that the leaves are brought to a point, as room must be left for further growth. The tie should be made a little higher than half-way up.

Cos lettuce can be sown outdoors from early March until August. They can also be sown under frame or cloche protection in the autumn or in February to provide an early cut.

Recommended varieties

CABBAGE VARIETIES: *Unrivalled* or *All the Year Round.* Can be sown outdoors from March to August in succession. These are favourite varieties for salads. *Webb's Wonderful.* A lettuce of large size. The leaves are crisp, crinkly and tender. Stands well during hot weather. *Buttercrunch.* One of the newer varieties with crisp and juicy leaves. Compact with large head. Stands well under drought conditions.

FRAME AND CLOCHE: Sow in mid-October. *May King* (syn. May Queen). One of the most successful varieties for this sowing. The outer leaves are sometimes tinged with red. *Ventura* (Elson's). A newer variety producing large heads in mid-April. *Attractie* (Unwin's). One of the best for autumn sowing and early spring production. *Premier* (Sutton's). A splendid variety for cloche and frame sowings. These are all cabbage lettuce.

Lobjoits Green. A splendid cos for underglass work and sowings in October or February.

COS VARIETIES: *Paris White.* A good summer variety for outdoor sowing from March until early August. Self-folding. *Balloon cos.* An immense lettuce for late spring or summer. It needs tying and should be grown on good soil and given ample supplies of water.

Chicory. Chicory is quickly becoming more popular for salad use and as it is available when other salad materials are scarce, it is well worth growing. The plants have a root that looks very much like a parsnip or an overgrown dandelion. During the winter the roots are forced into early growth and a large tight bud or chicon, as it is more properly called, is produced. This is some 6 in. long and is the edible portion, consisting of tightly folded leaves ivory-white in colour.

The crop is grown in the open on ground that has been manured for a previous crop. Seed is sown in shallow drills 12–15 in. apart in late May or June. The resultant seedlings are thinned out to stand at 9 in. apart. It is more than likely that one row will produce all the roots likely to be needed.

From November onwards the roots can be lifted as required and forced. Cut off any remaining leaves to within $\frac{1}{2}$ in. of the crown and shorten the roots to a uniform length of 7 in. by cutting off the lower portion. Select medium-sized roots of $1–1\frac{3}{4}$ in. in diameter. Large roots are liable to produce multiple heads and anything under 1 in. will not produce a worth-while chicon. Do not use fanged roots. Although the roots are fairly hardy it will be as well to draw up extra soil over those that are left in the ground during the winter.

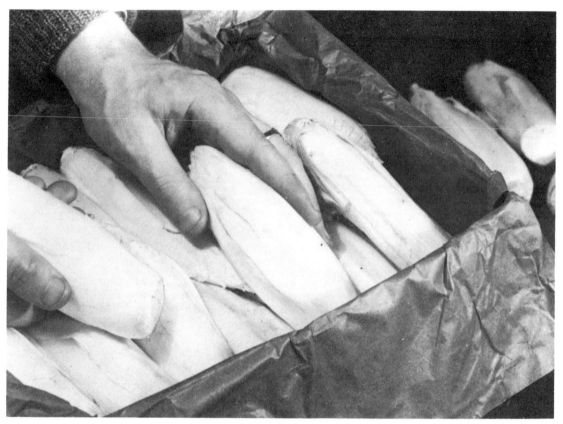

A market pack of forced chicory. A useful addition to the salad bowl during the dark days.

A convenient method of forcing is to partly fill a box with good garden soil to which peat has been added and having prepared the roots push them upright into the soil about 2 in. apart. Firm the soil round and between the roots with the fingers and add more soil until it is level with the crowns after firming. Now give a good watering via a fine rose.

Absolute darkness is essential in order to blanch the chicons and this can be done by inverting another box of similar size over the first. This must have both the top and bottom removed. Into the top box and over the watered roots place 7 or 8 in. of *dry* garden soil and place the whole under the staging in the greenhouse or bring it into the dwelling house. If there is a cellar or a warm garage this will do for no great heat is needed. Too much heat will, in fact, ruin the crop. If the boxes are large it would be better to carry out the work as near as possible to where forcing is to be done other-wise it will be difficult to move the boxes. A narrow strip of wood nailed on the ends of the top box will prevent it from slipping off if knocked or moved. Another method when only a few roots are to be forced is to set them in a large flower pot 2 in. apart and invert over them another pot of the same size. You cannot put soil in the top pot but you must cover up the drainage holes to make it light-proof. (*Figs. 20–21.*)

It will only be necessary to force a small number of roots at any one time but a continuity of supply can be maintained if roots are prepared and boxed at intervals of three weeks. It must be emphasized again that complete darkness is necessary or the chicons will become green and have a most unpleasant bitter taste. If any chicons push up though the soil before you want to cut them, cover them with a little more soil. The initial watering of the roots will be sufficient to supply them with moisture. Do not on any account water the covering soil.

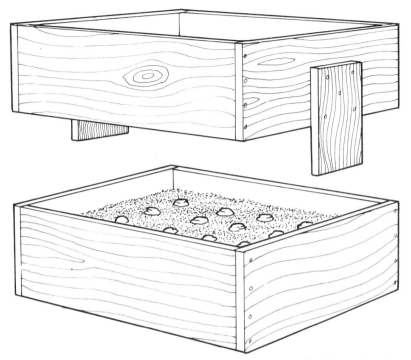

Fig. 20. Chicory roots set upright on the bottom box in soil. A bottomless box, if placed over this, will contain the dry soil to give a 7-in. cover to the roots.

Fig. 21. A forced chicon.

This will cause ugly markings on the chicons and may bring about rotting. A temperature of 10°C. (50°F.) is all that is required.

The chicons are ready when they are 6–7 in. long and are cut off immediately above the crown. Do not wash them but wipe off any soil or grit by wiping with a soft cloth from base to tip and do not leave them exposed to bright light before using.

Do not be content to accept just chicory seed. There is only one of three types of chicory that will produce the kind of chicon needed and that is Witloof, listed sometimes as White Witloof or Giant Witloof.

Endive. There are two main types of endive, the curled endive in which the leaves are finely divided and curled, and the Batavian endive which looks like a cos lettuce and is grown in the same way. The leaves are not divided but are somewhat curled. Curled endive is not very hardy but Batavian will stand up to all but the severest of frosts.

Curled endive for autumn use should be sown in June. Another sowing in early August will ensure a supply in late autumn and early winter. Seed is sometimes sown on a seed bed and the seedlings transplanted when they are 3 in. high.

A well-drained and fertile soil is needed to produce good endive and the surface should be worked down to a fine tilth. The sowing is made in shallow V-shaped drills 12 in. apart and the seedlings thinned to stand at 15 in. apart. Cultivation is the same as for lettuce.

Blanching is carried out during the late summer and on into the autumn and several methods are used. The leaves of the plants can be tied together as with cos lettuce or large flower pots can be inverted over the plants, taking care to place a tile or slate over the drainage hole. Yet another way of blanching is to lay a large slate or tile over the plant. Always wait until the plant is dry before covering in any way or heart rot may be brought about. Blanch only a few plants at one time, for once blanched the plants soon deteriorate.

In the autumn the plants can be lifted and replanted closely together in a well-darkened frame or they can be placed in a box and stood in a cellar or beneath the greenhouse staging, taking care to exclude light. Blan-

ching will take from three to four weeks. The endive for these sowings will not stand severe frost.

Batavian endive, being hardier, will provide heads during the late autumn and winter and should be sown in July and August. The plants should be thinned out to stand at 12 in. apart. This sowing is often made with a view to cloching during the harder weather and two rows can be sown under barn cloches, the rows being 10 in. apart.

When the plants are fully grown they must be blanched. The plants should be given a tie as with cos lettuce and our old friend the flower pot can be used to cover the plant, but it must be a large pot. Alternatively the plants can be lifted and replanted close together in the frame, which must be darkened. They can also be boxed and put in some conveniently darkened place. Cloches that have been well painted with dark distemper on the undersides of the glass form a very convenient method of blanching in situ. Two darkened ends will be needed. Two or three cloches will cover sufficient plants at one time.

Varieties suggested
  Exquisite Curled or Moss Curled.
  Round-Leaved Batavian.

Salad onions. Mention must be made here of salad or spring onions, for although they are often eaten as a separate dish they are more frequently used to add flavour and piquancy to the salad bowl. There is no need to go to any great lengths in preparing a bed as for bulb onions but they do, of course, need a fertile and well-cultivated soil. Most onions can be pulled as thinnings and used as salad onions, but the variety White Lisbon is far better for pulling green as there is no brown skin and the flavour is mild. Sowings can be made in August for pulling in the early spring and again in February for pulling during the early summer. Another sowing can be made during May if you want to continue the supply of young salad onions. There should be no need to do any thinning. The plants will not object to some shade during the summer and a sowing can be conveniently made between rows of peas etc.

A late January or February sowing made between lettuce in the frame or under cloches will provide very early pulling in the spring.

Varieties

White Lisbon. Easily the best variety for salad purposes. It is a quick grower and has a silver skin.

White Portugal. This is really one of the Spanish types but often used as a salad onion.

Radishes. Most people grow at least a few radishes for it is a crop that can be grown on any odd piece of ground that is vacant. But you can only expect to pull really succulent radishes from a soil that is rich in humus and finely worked, for they are only at their best when they are quickly grown. Most of the radishes needed will be sown as catch crops between other plants. Grown quickly on a soil that will be retentive of moisture, they will be tender and mild in flavour and totally undeserving of the rude things that are said about them.

Sowings can be made in drills $\frac{3}{4}$ in. deep, on a warm border in February and at intervals until September. Do not sow too many at one time. Just a pinch of seed every fortnight during the spring and summer. If you can manage to sow so that the seed is dropped at approximately inch intervals, little thinning will be needed.

Winter radishes can be bought as seed but are seldom grown in this country. China Rose is a good variety if you like a winter radish. The seeds should be sown in August and thinned to 6 in. apart. In November or December the roots can be lifted and stored in sand. The roots are from 4 to 6 in. long and are served sliced.

Varieties

French Breakfast. A variety suitable for early and later sowings. It is bright scarlet with a white tip and mild in flavour. *Scarlet Globe.* Of a brilliant red colour and globe shape. Suitable for either early or later sowings. *China Rose.* A winter variety for sowing in August. It is a large oval-shaped radish with scarlet skin and white flesh. It attains a length of 6 in. The flavour is on the strong side.

Mustard and cress. Another helpful ingredient for the salad and in demand for sandwiches and garnishing. It is better to sow the white mustard rather than the brown and it is really immaterial whether you sow the plain or curled cress as it is eaten in the seed-leaf stage.

M. and C. should be grown in boxes or seed-trays filled with good garden soil to which has been added a liberal amount of peat. Almost fill the tray and sift over enough finely sieved soil to complete the filling. Press this down with a piece of board or a presser and make quite level. The tray should now be given a good watering via a fine rose and stood to drain.

Sow the cress three days before the mustard as it takes a little longer to germinate. Sow very thickly over the whole surface and press down with a presser. Do not cover the seed with soil. If you cover with soil the M. and C. will be gritty. Put the tray in the dark or invert a box over it to keep off the light and keep it there until the stems have become an inch or more high and then bring it out into the light for a few days to let the leaves turn green. On no account water over the little seedlings for this will knock them all flat. If the tray needs watering (and it probably will not) immerse it in water almost to the rim. The water will come up from the bottom. Mustard and cress is ready to cut when it is 2 in. high. It is easiest to cut with a pair of scissors.

Corn salad. This is also known as lamb's lettuce and is a useful subject to help eke out salad supplies during the winter. As an ingredient to the salad it is not so well known in this country as on the Continent. The leaves are gathered like spinach.

Seed is sown from August to September to provide pickings in the late autumn and through the winter. Sow in rows 12 in. apart and thin out the plants to 6 in. Although it is hardly enough, the rows can be given cloche protection during the winter. This will ensure plenty of clean leaves free from grit and mud splashes or damaged by wind or heavy rain.

Variety

Round Leaved Corn Salad.

14 *Outdoor Tomatoes and Sweet Corn*

In northern parts of the country the outdoor cultivation of tomatoes must be looked on as being something of a gamble for one is at the mercy of whatever sort of weather we may have to contend with. The young plants are extremely frost-tender and quickly checked by cold winds and low temperatures. Even in the south it is unusual to plant out until towards the end of May or in early June.

It would need the whole of this book to do justice to the culture of the tomato, for it is a crop that amply repays the skill and time spent on it. Fortunately it is very accommodating and shows an adaptability that is surprising in a plant that originated in tropical America.

The soil for tomatoes must be in good heart but it is a mistake to dress with large quantities of fresh manure for the outdoor crop. The soil should be made fertile and retentive of moisture by the addition of old and well-rotted manure, peat and compost but drainage must be good. Get this work done well ahead of planting and a few days before planting is due give a dressing of some complete fertilizer with a high potash content and work this into the top few inches at the rate of 3 oz. per square yard.

If you can find a warm and sunny border under a wall or fence facing south or south-west that will do nicely, for the plants will be sheltered from cold winds and have the benefit of the warmth radiated from the wall or fence. This is not so necessary in the south and a more open position could be chosen, but it should not be unduly exposed. A position under a wall is liable to dry out, so take care to give ample water supplies to ensure that the plants do not suffer.

Where only a few plants are needed, it is better to buy them from a reliable nursery-man. Short jointed plants of a good colour and 8 or 9 in. high are needed. Refuse those leggy and weak-looking specimens sometimes offered and often stood outside the green-grocers' shops exposed to cold, searing winds. Plants such as these will not give you a return for your trouble, however much care you take. You can of course raise your own plants and this is an advantage, but you need a heated greenhouse and that is another story. It is possible, from a late sowing, to raise plants in the frame but they would be late.

The earliest planting in milder districts in the open will be during the last week in May or in early June. Plant with a trowel and avoid planting too deeply, the top of the soil ball should be just covered. If the plants are in pots, water them before planting them out. Firm planting is necessary and in order to support the plant against the wind push in a small bamboo cane nearby and tie the plant to this with a loose tie.

The ground between the plants should be kept hoed to maintain a loose surface and to keep down weed growth, and when the plants are being grown as cordons a stout stake should be given before they attain any great height. If the ground was well prepared before planting, little feeding will be needed but sometimes after the second truss has formed growth seems to slow up and a feed will then be needed. A recommended mixture is:

Sulphate of ammonia	3 parts	
Dried blood	2 parts	by weight
Superphosphate	7 parts	
Sulphate of potash	2 parts	

This should be scattered round the plants—approximately a dessertspoonful per plant.

Tomato, 'Moneymaker' (Stonors). Moderate sized fruits of good quality. Free from greenback and still one of the most popular varieties for the amateur.

Tomato, 'French Cross' (F_1 hybrid). A new bush variety suitable for cloche or frame cultivation or outdoor work. It is a heavy cropper and of good flavour. Photo: Messrs Sutton & Sons Ltd.

Or one of the proprietary tomato feeds can be used.

Side shoots should be removed as they appear. If you miss one and it becomes large cut it off close to the stem with a sharp knife. As the weather becomes warmer and possibly drier a mulch of leaf-mould, compost or lawn mowings along the rows will help maintain the cool and moist root-run that tomato plants enjoy. About mid-August or when four trusses have set the plant should be stopped by pinching out the growing shoot two leaves beyond the last truss. This will direct the energy of the plant towards swelling the fruits rather than producing more and more leaves and fruits that have no chance of attaining any size or ripening.

Do not overwater but endeavour to keep the soil nicely moist. A sudden flooding after a dry spell will bring about split fruit. An occasional spraying over with aired water will help the flowers to set. After the first two trusses have set the bottom leaves may turn yellow and these should be removed by bending the leaf up towards the stem until it snaps off at the joint. This will allow a better passage of air round the plants. Leaves higher up the plant should not be removed unless they have become large and are shading the fruit unduly. A leaf here and there can be removed, but remember that the leaves are the food factory of the plant and to take off too many is to drastically cut down the food supply and the energy that produces the fruits.

As with potatoes, tomatoes are liable to blight. Spraying with a copper fungicide is of more use as a means of prevention than a cure against this disease, so spray several times during the season giving the first spray towards the end of July. Spray with a bent extension on the sprayer or use one with a

The well-known 'Amateur' tomato. Another bush variety that needs no staking and very suitable for the small garden. Photo: Messrs W. L. Unwin Ltd.

bent nozzle so that the undersides as well as the top of the leaves can be well covered.

Under cloches. Cloches can be used to advantage where tomato growing is concerned. They will permit the plants to be got out a month ahead of normal planting. Mid-April is the usual date for planting out under cloches in the south and in more northern districts the opportunity of extending the all too short season of growth, both in the spring and in the early autumn, makes tomato growing in those districts possible.

The plants are set out in the normal way 18 in. apart in a single row. The cloches must be removed when the foliage reaches the top of the cloche, when the plants should be provided with stout stakes and grown on in the normal way as outdoor plants. In the early autumn the stakes are removed and the plants laid down on straw and re-covered with cloches to finish ripening any green tomatoes that are left. A spraying against blight should be given before re-cloching.

By growing one of the bush or dwarf types the plants can be set out early and cloched throughout the season using a large cloche. These will need neither staking nor pruning. Polythene tunnels are very useful for starting off and protecting the plants in the early days, but the material should be raised on one side whenever possible to allow ventilation.

A variety of tomato that does well in one district may not do nearly so well in another. There are many varieties available and in addition to studying the seed lists, the grower should have a word with a gardening neighbour who may be able to help in the choice of a variety suited to the district.

The cultivation of tomatoes by the ring culture method has aroused considerable interest over the last few years. This method can be adapted to outdoor growing and has met with considerable success in gardens where for various reasons tomato growing was thought to be impossible.

A trench 5–6 in. deep is taken out and the bottom left level. The soil is replaced with an aggregate of small ash, gravel, fine breeze or finely broken bricks. On this, bottomless pots or 'rings' filled with a good potting compost are stood 18 in. apart. The young tomato plants are planted in the rings.

If the aggregate is kept well watered roots will quickly find their way into it, thus forming a two-zone root system. The principle is that if a weekly or bi-weekly feed is given via the rings and all the water needed given via the aggregate the two root systems will be independent of the garden soil; one being concerned with supplying the plants with nutrients and the other with moisture. If the trench is lined with polythene the aggregate will be isolated from the surrounding soil. A few slits in the polythene will permit drainage. (*Fig. 22*)

The varieties given below have, to the writer's knowledge, given general satisfaction in many parts of the country.

Recommended varieties

Alicante. A modern and early variety of nice size that does well both under glass and in the open. *Harbinger.* Very suitable for sowing under cloches. A heavy cropper of medium-size fruits. *Moneymaker.* An old Stoner variety that is excellent for outdoor growing and free from greenback. The fruits are rather slow to colour. *Market King.* A splendid cropper and a great favourite in the Midlands and the north. *Amateur.* A bush variety that ripens very early. The fruits are of medium size and early. *Sleaford Abundance.* A bush variety that stands well. It is early and the fruits of medium size. These two varieties are very suitable for outdoor or cloche protection and need neither staking nor pruning.

Sweet corn. It was during the last war that sweet corn began to be grown more freely in this country. Being frost-tender the season of growth did not allow time for the development of the cobs. With the introduction of the John Innes Hybrid, cultivation became possible for that variety, which is still one of the best for early work, combining the good qualities of a maincrop with the advantages of a more hardy and earlier variety. Sweet corn is a form of maize but it must not be

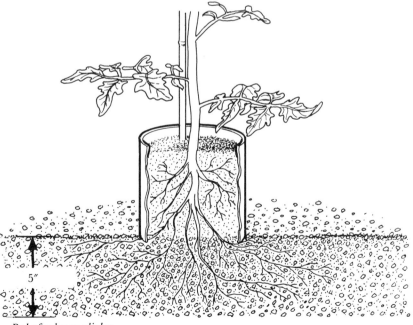

5″

Bed of ashes or clinker

Fig. 22. Ring culture of tomatoes.

A promising crop of sweet corn. Sown under cloches in mid-April.

confused with the maize that is fed to animals. Sweet corn has a much higher sugar content than any other type. It is now grown in private gardens in many parts of the country and served in many ways. Cooked and taken off the cob it makes an interesting addition to a salad.

A usual method of growing is to sow in mild heat in April in small pots and plant out at the end of May or early June. The plants resent transplanting and great care must be taken to keep the young plants watered until they are established. Seeds of an early variety can be sown outdoors towards the end of May in the more southern

half of the country. Almost any soil that is in good heart will grow sweet corn but plenty of organic matter such as old manure or compost is needed on the lighter soils. Before planting or sowing give a 4-oz. per square yard dressing of a complete fertilizer.

It is better to sow or plant several short rows in a block rather than one long row. This will assist pollination as the pollen is very fine and will blow away with the least wind instead of falling on the silks of the embryo cob. Cobs with only a few seeds are due to poor pollination.

Sow the seeds 15 in. apart in drills 1–1½ in. deep and 15 in. apart. If you have seed to spare drop in two seeds per station and retain the best of the two seedlings.

There is little to do during the growing season other than keeping the ground hoed and seeing that the plants do not suffer from lack of moisture. As the plants grow, buttress roots will grow out from the base of the stem. These help to anchor the plants firmly and when hoeing, soil should be drawn up to the plants to encourage these roots to form. At this time a mulch of leaves, compost or lawn mowings will help to maintain a moist root-run. The tillers or side shoots that appear at the base of the plant can be left. It is quite natural for them to form, and there is no need to remove them.

Each plant will produce two good cobs but it is not easy to know just when to take them. In early August one should expect the first cobs. Look first at the silks that hang from the tips of the cobs. When these have withered and turned brown the sheath covering the cob should be parted to expose the seeds and one of the seeds squeezed with the two thumb nails. If a watery fluid is exuded the cob is not ready; a thicker milky fluid indicates readiness for cutting, while a thick creamy substance will show that the cob is past its prime. If you note the state of the silks on the cob that is just right others can be cut when they have the same appearance. When the cob becomes ready the husk loses its damp, clammy feeling and has a certain degree of harshness when felt. The cobs should be cut in the early morning and placed in a cool, dark place. Undue exposure to light after cutting will result in part of the sugar content being turned to starch. The cobs should be cooked and eaten as soon after cutting as possible.

Undoubtedly the best and surest way to grow sweet corn is to sow under cloches where the crop is to mature, using one of the early hybrid varieties. The sowing can be made in mid-April, the seeds being spaced at staggered intervals of 15 in. apart. Two rows can be sown 12 in. apart under barn cloches and the cloches removed when frost danger has passed. Gardeners in the north will need to defer the sowing for a week or two and of course the cobs will be a little later than in the south but the earlier sowing will give a longer growing period for development and good cobs can be had. In the south a sowing under cloches should produce cobs towards the end of July. An outdoor sowing in May in the more southern districts of one of the maincrop varieties will carry on a succession if required.

Varieties suggested

North Star (F_1 hybrid). A new hybrid variety producing early cobs 7–8 in. long. Does well under adverse conditions. *John Innes Hybrid.* An early and vigorous hybrid but of compact growth. Excellent for early cloche work or later sowing. *Golden Bantam.* An early maincrop variety. Hardy and producing medium-sized cobs of excellent flavour. This is the variety largely grown for canning. *Extra Early Sweet* (Thompson and Morgan). A new F_1 hybrid that is very early and has a sugar content said to be higher than any other sweet corn. Specially recommended for the north and those districts where the season of growth is short.

15 Cucumbers, Marrows and Courgettes

Ridge cucumbers can be grown outdoors during the summer with little trouble, and newer and re-selected varieties are less prickly and of better shape than the older varieties. The best have skins almost as smooth as a frame cucumber and are certainly easier to grow and more hardy.

The earliest plants must be raised in a greenhouse or heated frame and the seed should be sown in small pots. The plants can be set out early in May under cloches and by the end of the month or in early June they can be planted out in the open. Three seeds can be sown in situ in late May or early June and the best plant retained. Plants should be set 2 ft. 6 in. apart. In more exposed districts planting must wait another week or two.

Where only two or three plants are to be grown it is better to take out holes a foot deep and approximately 18 in. across and nearly fill it with fermenting material. A 6-in. layer of good garden soil and compost is placed over this in the form of a low mound and, after watering well, the seeds or plant set on this.

There is no need to do a lot of training with ridge cucumbers. Simply pinch out the growing point when it has six or seven leaves to induce branching. Give plenty of water and feed with liquid manure. Syringe over with clear water on dry and warm evenings; this will help the plants and discourage red spider. It must be admitted that ridge cucumbers are somewhat of a gamble other than in the more favoured districts but nevertheless are well worth while during a good summer.

The garden frame can be put to good use in the summer by growing a cucumber of the frame variety. From the frame you can have the long cucumbers such as you find in the shops, but they will not always be as straight and the underside may be a little pale, but the cucumbers will taste just as good.

Sow the seeds separately in 3-in. pots in the greenhouse. A nice open potting compost is needed to fill the pots but do not firm it. Fill the pot and push in the seed sideways $\frac{3}{4}$ to 1 in. deep. Give the bottom of the pot a gentle knock on the bench to settle the compost and water via a fine rose. Cover with a piece of glass. In a temperature of 20°C. (68°F.) germination will be had in three or four days. Remove the glass when the leaves push through and shade from bright sun. Keep the compost nicely moist. The sowing should be made four weeks before the anticipated sowing date.

During the waiting period the bed can be prepared. To economize on manure and compost make a hole as already described about 15 in. deep and 18 in. wide and partly fill this with manure or compost. Some lawn mowings can be added. Over this place 5 or 6 in. of good potting compost. Some old turf chopped up into small pieces can be mixed in with this. Bring the whole up into the shape of a low mound and plant on top of the mound. Have the light on the frame for a few days beforehand to warm up the soil. Plant with a trowel and provide some shade. A little extra bone meal added to the compost will be all to the good.

When the plant has made four or five leaves pinch out the growing point and train the resultant laterals towards the corners of the frame. When they have almost reached the limit they will need pinching back and sub-laterals will quickly grow. On these the fruits will form and the fruiting shoot should be pinched off two leaves beyond the fruits. Do not allow the frame to become overcrowded but cut back unwanted laterals to two leaves and also cut back any non-fruiting shoots.

Cucumbers must have a humid atmosphere. This can be maintained in the frame by watering the plant and by spraying over with aired water once or twice a day and by careful ventilation. Take care to spray over the whole area of the frame. The plants will need ample water but avoid watering immediately round the stem as any water-logging at this point may cause stem rot or canker. Do not overdo the watering for a wet bed will also be a cold one and the soil in which the plant is growing should be nicely warm and moist. Except on very hot evenings close the frame after watering in the early evening but during the day a chink of air should be left, and increased a little during the hotter weather. The plant will need a light shading and a dressing of dried blood should be given fortnightly. When roots show on the surface of the soil top dress with more rich soil.

Cucumbers do not need pollinating so pick off male flowers. A fertilized fruit will be bitter and 'bull-nosed'. The female flower will be recognized by the embryo behind the flower.

Suggested varieties

Butcher's Disease-Resisting (frame).

Telegraph (frame).

Conqueror. Will do well under somewhat less humid conditions than others (frame).

Perfection Ridge. An almost spineless ridge cucumber.

King of the Ridge. Another almost smooth variety.

Vegetable marrow. It must be admitted that marrows are not a favourite vegetable with everybody. Perhaps the lack of popularity is due somewhat to the fact that so often they are left to grow too large and then served 'plain boiled'. Many people do not know what a young and small marrow can taste like when served with an appropriate sauce. The monstrous specimens sent to Harvest Festivals as a thank-offering are no criterion although these will make a most delicious preserve—if you like ginger.

There are two main classes of marrows—the trailing and the bush. The old method of growing trailing marrows was on a heap but to do so now would be to court failure for in

A well matched pair of vegetable marrows. The variety is 'Green Bush'. Photo: Messrs Sutton & Sons Ltd.

Vegetable marrow plants for early cropping in the frame or under cloches must be raised in the greenhouse The plant pictured is nearly ready for planting out.

those days the large heaps over which the plant grew were heaps of surplus manure which had been stacked to mature and provided just the right conditions for the trailing marrow. Any heap today would be little more than a hump in a small garden and would quickly dry out. In the smaller gardens of today the best plan is to grow marrows on the flat in order to economize in manure or compost and space and grow one of the bush varieties. It is better therefore to prepare stations as already described for cucumbers. Into the hole put as much manure or compost as you can spare and make up bulk by adding leaf-mould and lawn mowings. With the covering soil add a good handful of some complete fertilizer such as fish manure or Growmore.

For the earliest cutting the seed is sown during the second week in March in the heated greenhouse and the plants will be ready to go out under cloches or in the frame during the second or third week in April. Under cloches they should be planted at 3 ft. apart. The cloches can be removed during the third week in May and young marrows will be available from towards the end of June.

Outdoor planting must wait until frost danger has passed. In the south this should be in late May or early June but in northern gardens the second week in June would be a safer date. Seed can be sown in situ from towards the end of May on prepared stations. Sow three or four seeds per station and thin down to one plant. A large pot or

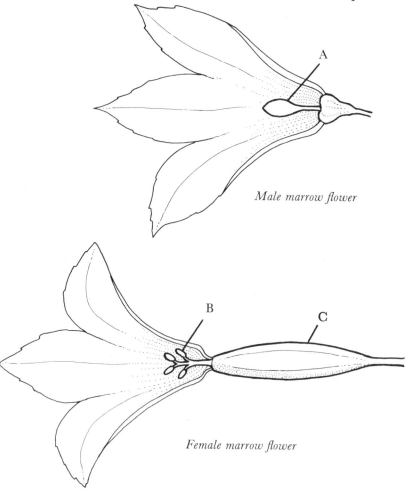

Male marrow flower

Female marrow flower

Fig 23. Pollen must be transferred from the pistil of the male flower (A) to the stamens of the female (B). C. Embryo marrow.

glass jar would help germination and would be put over the young seedlings if frost was forecast. As soon as the young marrows are seen to be growing a fortnightly feed of liquid manure or dried blood can be given. Plenty of water will be needed to maintain the warm and moist root-run needed. It is dryness at the roots or lack of pollination that causes the embryo marrows to yellow and fall off and hand pollination may be necessary in the early days to ensure a set (*Fig. 23*).

Marrows should be cut and eaten when they are 10–12 in. long if you want them at their best.

'Sutton's Courgette' (*F*₁ *hybrid*). *The fruits should be cut when 4 to 5 in. long. Photo: Messrs Sutton & Sons Ltd.*

Varieties suggested

White or Green Bush. These do not crop so heavily as the trailing types but take up less room.

Table Dainty. An early trailing variety producing small fruits of good quality.

Courgette. This marrow-like vegetable looks like a tiny marrow and is becoming very popular, especially with those who have sampled it abroad. It has a flavour not unlike asparagus and the small fruits are cooked and served whole and unpeeled. It is delicious when boiled and served with butter or a white sauce. It is also served fried in butter or oil. The fruits are cut when they are 4–6 in. long and the plants crop heavily over a long period when cut regularly. The leaves of the plant are a little more divided than the marrow.

Courgettes are raised and grown in exactly the same way as marrows and under cloche form a useful crop for early summer. Like marrows they are frost-tender and must not be planted out without protection until frosts are no longer likely. The ground in which they are grown should be generously manured with organic material and the plants spaced at 2 ft. apart. A true courgette should be sown.

Variety suggested

Sutton's Courgette (F_1 hybrid).
Courgette (True French).

16 Some miscellaneous and more unusual vegetables

There are a number of unusual vegetables but few of them are really popular and are therefore seldom grown. It is not proposed to give a long list of them here but merely to mention a few that could be of interest.

Jerusalem artichoke. This is by no means unknown or unusual but it is convenient to include it in this chapter. Some people like them while other loathe the sight of them, because the old strains so often left in established gardens are apt to turn black in the cooking and also they are very knobbly and difficult to prepare. The modern white strains offered by the seedsmen today are very much nicer to eat than the old purple strains and are of better shape, so if you are contemplating growing artichokes be sure to obtain a modern white strain.

The Jerusalem artichoke has nothing whatever to do with Jerusalem or the Jews for it hails from Canada where it was used by the Indians as a vegetable. The plants grow to a great height—some 9 ft. or more—and make a very good screen or windbreak, but towards the end of the summer stout stakes and wire may be needed to give some support or strong winds may blow the plants over.

Artichokes will grow on any type of soil so long as it is not too wet. The site should be dug over and manured and planting can be done in February or early March. The tubers are set at 1 ft. apart and 6 in. deep. Each row should be 2 ft. 6 in. apart.

The tubers are often left in the ground and lifted as they are required but it is better to lift the whole crop and store them in sand before the winter is too far advanced. Dig them out as you would potatoes and take care to remove every tiny tuber or you will have trouble the next season, as every piece of root will grow.

The only true artichoke is the globe artichoke. These make truly noble plants and it is the scales of the large immature flower buds that are eaten.

It is possible to propagate from seed but the more usual method is to remove suckers with a sharp knife in April or May and plant these out 3 ft. apart. If more than a few plants are to be grown the rows should be given a spacing of 4 ft. Good fertile ground is needed if large buds are to be produced.

It is a crop that takes up a great deal of room for a long time and provides little in the way of food, and is therefore unsuitable for a small garden.

Celeriac. As far as flavour is concerned celeriac can be used as a substitute for celery and is far easier to grow. It is the swollen turnip-like root that is eaten. The root can be boiled or sliced and eaten raw. It is also used in salads.

Sow in a warm greenhouse during March, prick out and, after hardening off, plant out in the open at 12 in. apart in late May or June on fertile ground. There is no need to make trenches or earth it up. Remove any basal growths and keep the plant growing on a single stem. In dry weather ample water supplies must be given otherwise the root will be tough and woody.

The roots should be lifted in late October when the leaves have yellowed. These old leaves should be removed with the exception of the centre tuft and the roots stored in sand in a cool place.

Kohl rabi. This rather unusual vegetable is grown in large quantities on the Continent where it is quite popular. Of the two types grown, the green is more tender than the purple. It is a large rounded root very similar to a turnip but has leaves which develop over the surface. Like turnips it belongs to the cruciferae group and should be grown with the brassicas.

Seed is sown from mid-March to early July and finally thinned to stand at 6 in. between the plants. The crop is treated in the same way as turnips.

Mercury or Good King Henry. This has long been grown in the kitchen garden as a substitute for asparagus and is popular in parts of Lincolnshire.

Seeds may be sown in situ during April or May in rows 2 ft. apart and the plants thinned out and left at 18 in. apart. Seeds are also sown in boxes and the seedlings planted out when large enough. It is possible to divide up old roots. If planted on good fertile soil it crops heavily and during the summer the leaves may be used as spinach. It produces a large number of shoots that can be blanched by earthing up the plant. The shoots can be tied up in small bundles and cooked like asparagus.

Pumpkins and Gourds. These belong to the same family as melons, marrows and cucumbers and all need somewhat similar treatment. They are grown in the open like the marrows for they do not object so strongly to cooler and less humid conditions but they all like a well-manured soil, for they are gross feeders.

The plants are raised under glass as described in a previous chapter for ridge cucumbers and marrows or later in the season seeds can be sown on prepared stations. Pumpkins and squashes are native to America where they are much more popular than in this country. Pumpkins will grow to a great size and weight and specimens up to one hundredweight are mentioned, but you will be lucky if you get one over half that weight. King of the Mammoths is a very large pumpkin and seed can be had from most seedsmen if you think of growing one for 'the largest pumpkin' class.

The gourds are very ornamental and useful for winter decoration, many being of curious shapes and various colours. The Hubbard Squash is one of the best of the squashes for eating and can be had under that name from all seedsmen. In itself the pumpkin has little flavour although rather sweeter than the marrow. Unless it is cooked with apples, fruit and lemon it will be disappointing.

New Zealand Spinach. This is looked on as a substitute for spinach but it has little to commend itself, although the leaves lack the bitterness of spinach and it has the merit of withstanding heat and will often thrive on light and dry soils where spinach would rapidly seed and die. It is tender and must be raised under glass in late March or April and planted out in late May. It spreads very rapidly and needs lots of room, so plant it at 3 ft. each way.

The shoots are pinched off and cooked as spinach. Although it will withstand dry weather it will provide more shoots, which will be more tender, if it is well watered during dry spells.

Salsify. This is a vegetable grown for its roots, which are in season during the winter. Because of its fleshy roots it is sometimes known as the vegetable oyster. It should be grown in well cultivated soil that has been manured for a previous crop and no fresh manure should be used as the roots 'fang' easily.

Seed is sown in April. The drills should be 12 in. apart and $\frac{3}{4}$ in. deep. Early thinning is necessary and the seedlings first thinned to 4 in. and finally to 8 in. apart. The only attention needed will be thinning out and keeping the hoe going during the summer.

The parsnip-like roots can be used in late autumn and during the winter. Like parsnips they can be left in the ground and lifted as required or they can be lifted and stored. It should be remembered that if damaged the roots will bleed like beetroot.

17 Herbs

The herb garden and the gathering and drying of the leaves and shoots for winter use was once the responsibility of the lady of the house. Medicinal, culinary and sweetly-scented herbs were all grown and freely used and the housewife would seem to have had a pretty busy time in those days. The herb garden has long since disappeared and the chief interest now lies in what are sometimes known as the 'big four', namely mint, parsley, sage and thyme. With a few exceptions little use is made of culinary herbs other than these but it would be as well here to mention two or three of these useful but lesser known herbs for the names at least will be familiar.

Mint. There are several kinds of mint available but that known as spearmint is more generally grown and used in making mint sauce. The round-leaved mint is said to be of better flavour but the leaves are somewhat hairy and the plants become rather tall and for these reasons are not so acceptable.

Roots of spearmint can be purchased or obtained from a kindly neighbour but ensure that they are not affected with rust. Spearmint is very susceptible to this trouble so do not accept roots from an affected bed. Rust can be recognized by the presence of orange-coloured pustules on the base of the stems and spores on the undersides of the leaves. Sort out the roots into short strips and lay them in drills 2 in. deep, spacing the drills at a fair distance apart as the creeping roots will soon cover the available space. The bed should be of good rich soil and the ideal position would be in partial shade on a ground retentive of moisture.

The roots of mint are great travellers and unless some control is exercised it will over-run the garden in a year or two. One method to control its rapid encroachment is to build a wall around the bed 1 ft. in depth using old bricks or thin concrete blocks. Another method is to sink an old galvanized bath in the ground and fill this with good soil and plant in this, but do not forget to cut the bottom out or make plenty of holes for drainage purposes. It is best to make a new bed every two or three years. Just lift a few roots in the spring and plant them elsewhere.

The availability of this much-used herb can be extended into the late autumn if a portion of the bed is covered with a cloche or two and in the early part of the year when the bed is cleaned up the odd cloche will encourage early shoots. Cover in the ends of the cloches to form a handlight. Roots can be planted in a box and placed in the frame in January to provide early shoots.

It is more convenient to grow mint and parsley as near to the back door as possible, which makes it easy to pop out to gather a leaf of parsley or a sprig of mint, especially on a wet day.

Parsley. This herb is always in great demand for sauces and garnishing. It is invaluable during the winter and the early spring as supplies are always short. Like mint it needs a deep moist soil but you will not need a long row across the garden. It makes a good edging but otherwise a dozen plants will be ample for most households.

Parsley seed is sown during March to provide supplies during the summer and again in July for picking in the winter and early spring. It has the reputation of being the slowest of the vegetable seeds to germinate but if moist conditions are given it will germinate more quickly. Do not despair if three weeks pass and no seedlings appear.

Thin out the seedlings first to 3 in. and finally to 9 in. Good spacing will produce large and sturdy plants.

You can make sure of good clean parsley during the winter by cloching a few plants in November or by transplanting into the frame.

Champion Moss Curled is a favourite variety to grow and has tightly curled leaves with long stems. *Myatt's Garnishing* is another good variety, being a little more compact.

Sage. The leaves of this small shrubby plant are used with other herbs for stuffing. There are two main kinds, the green and the red. Green sage has velvety and somewhat wrinkled round leaves while red sage has dark-reddish narrow leaves. It is the green and round-leaf sage that is wanted.

Sage can be raised from seed but it is far better to buy plants initially and keep up the stock by means of cuttings. The plants should be set out at 18 in. apart in spring. Cuttings can be taken in May with a 'heel' (i.e. the shoot should be removed with a piece of the old wood attached). The cuttings, which should be 2 in. long, are inserted in sandy soil when they will soon root. When they are 4–5 in. long the tips should be nipped out to induce a more bushy habit. If the shoots are stood in the frame they will root a little quicker.

Sage plants soon become straggling and untidy and should be re-newed every three years. A dressing of some complete fertilizer given in the spring will be beneficial.

Thyme. Like sage, thyme does best in light well-drained soil. The two types that concern us here are the common thyme and the lemon thyme. Young plants can be had from a nursery or you may be able to beg some from a gardening friend. The plants should be set out in the spring. Seed can be sown of the common thyme but it does not come true to type and it is far better to propagate by means of cuttings taken in the early summer or by division of the old roots. The ground should be given a dressing of lime before planting out.

The plants are prone to become leggy and untidy as they age and renewal is necessary every two or three years. Set the plants 15 in. apart. Thyme also makes a very useful edging.

Lemon thyme is a rather smaller plant, the leaves of which have a refreshing but rather strong scent of lemon—a scent that can conjure up a picture of old-fashioned gardens rich with herbs, fragrant shrubs and old-fashioned flowers. Lemon thyme can be mixed in with the common thyme when drying and storing for winter use.

Horseradish. If you can still afford a joint of beef horseradish sauce is the compliment to it. Horseradish, if it is to be grown at all should be well grown and not neglected or relegated to the rubbish corner where it will be completely starved and only produce thin and whippy roots. If horseradish is given deeply dug and well-manured ground long and thick thongs or roots will be produced which will be straight and of good flavour and easier to grate.

Start by buying straight roots in February or March and plant them on well-prepared ground. Plant in short rows 15 in. apart and set the roots or thongs upright 9 in. apart in the rows. Horseradish is often left undisturbed for many years and becomes hopelessly overcrowded and starved and the roots not worth the digging. It should be dug up every alternate year and the bed replanted after taking out every piece of root and manuring the ground. Any thin useless roots should be discarded. Select straight roots 8 or 9 in. long each with a bud and replant.

Roots can also be dug in the autumn and stored in damp sand for use in the kitchen or replanting the next spring.

Fennel. The leaves of fennel are used to flavour sauces served with fish and the feathery foliage is sometimes used for garnishing. Seed can be sown in April or May or old roots can be divided in the spring to increase the stock. The plants should be set out at 12 in. apart. A fertile soil is needed to produce good fennel. Fennel would seem to be more popular in the north than in the south.

Tarragon. This herb is used chiefly as a flavour for vinegar and is sometimes added to a salad. A light and well-drained position is needed where it will get plenty of sunlight. The stems are woody and grow to a height of 3 ft. Roots can be purchased and planted in April 18 in. apart. The soil should be kept nicely moist until the plant is established.

It can be propagated by means of cuttings or root divisions in the spring. Root the cuttings in sandy soil in a frame.

Marjoram. There are several kinds of marjoram but we are only concerned with two—the sweet marjoram and the pot marjoram. The sweet marjoram is really a perennial but it is not hardy and is usually treated as a half-hardy annual. Seeds are sown in boxes in March in a little warmth and pricked out into other boxes at 3 in. apart. The plants can be set out at 6 in. apart during May or early June in the open. Seed can also be sown outdoors in May, pricked off and finally set out at 6 in. apart. Sweet marjoram must be raised annually.

The pot marjoram is a perennial which you can buy and plant in the spring or you can raise it from seed. The plants can be left undisturbed for three or four years. A better and quicker way to propagate is to pull away pieces from the plant with some roots attached and plant these 9 in. apart. The dried leaves should consist of a mixture of both kinds.

Marjoram plants should be kept on the moist side or the leaves will yellow and become useless.

18 *Pests and diseases*

A formidable list of pests and diseases could be given that might well be calculated to discourage any prospective vegetable grower. Fortunately most of them would rarely be met with and the list can consist of those more common and most likely to be encountered. One must remember, however, that in general good cultivation methods, correct sowing and spacing will result in a better and healthier plant. Such a plant is less likely to suffer than one which is late in season or struggling for existence because of poor cultivation, and a plethora of insecticides and fungicides will not compensate for poor husbandry. Once established most pests and diseases spread rapidly and so it is essential that control is effected as soon as any trouble appears.

Soil pests such as *leather-jackets* and *wireworm* often follow the breaking of old pasture but they gradually disappear with cultivation. In the meantime wireworm dust can be used to limit them. Both feed on the roots of plants and wireworms can be a serious pest under these conditions. *Millipedes* are soil creatures feeding on vegetable matter, sluggish in movement and coiling themselves into a circle when disturbed. Wireworm dust or trapping with grapefruit or orange skins can be effective. *Slugs* and *snails* attack most plants but are too common to need any description. Control is with slug bait. *Woodlice* are dark grey creatures apparently scaly and often associated with rotting wood. Their greatest sphere of activity seems to lie in enlarging damage that other pests have initiated. Always ensure that vegetable debris and other rotting material is cleared away and if woodlice are troublesome dust with wireworm dust.

Asparagus. The foliage of asparagus is sometimes attacked by a black and yellow beetle or its larvae of about $\frac{3}{8}$ in. length. Derris dust or spray will control it. When affected the foliage should be burnt when it is cut down in the autumn.

Beetroot is sometimes attacked by the *mangold fly*. The larvae of this fly burrow into the leaves like a leaf-miner and can cripple a young plant. Nicotine as a dust or spray is probably the best control. *Flea beetle* is a serious pest of brassica seedlings but may also attack beetroot. The beetles notch the edges of the young leaves, often completely crippling them. The pest is worse in hot, dry weather. Derris dust or spray should control them. See also under 'Brassica'.

Brassica (cabbages, cauliflowers, Brussels sprouts etc.). These crops are often attacked by a grey waxy aphid known as *mealy cabbage aphis*. When spraying against them considerable force is needed and if possible a spreading agent such as soft soap should be used in the spray. Other types of aphis will also attack brassicas but Malathion forms an excellent control for all types. *Cabbage root fly*. This is a pest which does damage by tunnelling into the roots of plants from the seedling stage onward. The entire plants will probably collapse and on removal from the soil little grubs will be seen on roots and stem. B.H.C. as a drench, dip or dust to the soil around the plant is effective and should always be used where the trouble is known to exist. *Flea beetles* can be numerous on brassica seedlings and must be controlled. Dusting with Derris should prove satisfactory. *Cabbage white fly*. These are tiny creatures which fly off the plants when they are disturbed. Malathion as a dust or spray will give control. In the case of Brussel sprouts it must be done early in order to prevent damage to the sprout button.

Club root. This is a soil-borne disease which attacks roots and stem causing large malformations, and plants attacked seldom succeed. The disease can remain in the ground for many years and wide rotations should be practised. Where the disease is known to exist brassica plants can be given some protection by puddling the roots in calomel before planting or by dusting a little calomel in each planting hole. If possible avoid planting any of the brassicas on affected ground for several years—this includes turnips. Affected ground should be given a good dressing of lime.

Caterpillars. Different kinds of caterpillars will be seen. The cabbage white has been known to skeletonize whole fields of brassicas. These are easily dealt with either in a small way by hand picking and crushing the eggs or by at least two sprayings or dusting with Derris.

Carrots. *Carrot fly* is a serious pest in some districts and seed should be dressed with a proprietary seed dressing. Later sowings often escape the main carrot fly attack, which occurs in May and June. Never leave thinnings lying on the ground. Whizzed naphthalene dusted along the rows will act as a deterrent by disguising the carrot scent. Always compress the soil after thinning.

Celery. The maggot of the *celery fly* can seriously cripple celery by tunnelling into the leaves. This creature can be seen within a pale brown area of the leaf. It can be controlled with Malathion dust or spray. *Carrot fly* can also affect celery but dusting with carrot fly dust around the plants will check this. Should aphids be troublesome Malathion will soon clear them. The disease *leaf spot* cripples the leaves, which become brown in patches with little black spots. This is controlled by spraying with Zineb or by dressing the seed with Thiram.

Cucumber (frame). The worst pest of frame cucumbers is *red spider*. These are pale yellow pinhead size spiders feeding mainly on the undersides of the leaves. The pest is a crippling one. Moist conditions without undue heat plus a little shading usually keep the pest at bay but if you have to spray use a Malathion spray. This will also control any aphids or white fly which may be present.

Lettuce and Endive. *Aphids* are the main pest but Malathion given early will control it although once the lettuce has started to heart it is necessary to use a systemic insecticide such as Rogor. *Cutworms*, the larvae of certain moths, may attack the root at about soil level, often severing the stem and bringing about complete collapse. They may be found in the soil around a wilting plant and should be dealt with. Hand picking over the small clods of soil round the plant will reveal them. The creatures feed at night. Hoe regularly between plants. Paris green and bran can be used as a poison bait where it is safe to do so. Good cultivation and clean land usually limit this pest.

Botrytis (greymould). This fungus disease may attack lettuce and unless checked will cause collapse. In severe cases the head rots off at the base. Folosan is an effective control and should be dusted over small seedlings as an insurance against an attack. Thiram will also give some control.

Mint. This herb is often attacked by an orange-coloured rust. Affected roots can be cleared of disease during dormancy by immersing in warm water at 110°F. for 10 minutes. There does not seem to be any cure for the summer stages of the disease.

Onions. *Onion fly* is the worse pest of onions and again this is a pest which attacks the base and roots of the plants causing collapse. A Thiram seed dressing should be used where onion fly is known to be prevalent. Use whizzed naphthalene as a repellent and to disguise the onion scent. *Downy mildew.* This is a disease which attacks the foliage, giving it a grey appearance with collapse of the leaf tissue. Zineb should be used at the first signs. *White rot* is a soil-borne disease which rots out the base of the bulb and when known to be prevalent in the neighbourhood calomel dust should be used as a dressing or as a puddle before planting.

Peas and Beans. Aphids, particularly black ones, can be a serious pest on these crops but here again Malathion provides an effective control. *Weevils* eat out semi-circular holes at the edges of the leaves. They are not very serious on these crops and dusting with Derris will control them. Grubs are sometimes found in the mature pods. These are the larvae of the *pea moth* and could have been controlled by spraying with Derris after a good set had been obtained; an example of prevention rather than cure. *Red spider* may be troublesome on runner beans under hot and dry conditions but plenty of moisture applied over the foliage should keep it within bounds. *Thrips* cause a silvery scar and twisted pea pods. This can be controlled with Malathion. *Chocolate spot*, a form of the disease *Botrytis*, can be troublesome on broad beans particularly in cold and wet conditions. Spraying with Bordeaux mixture will help but as with other diseases rotation of crops is the best method of avoiding future trouble. *Powdery mildew* may attack peas particularly late-sown ones but Karathane is an excellent control for this trouble.

Potatoes. *Potato Blight* is the worse trouble where potatoes are concerned. This starts as a small black area in the leaf and quickly spreads until the foliage collapses. The disease spores may wash into the soil and affect the tubers where it eventually shows as a black rotting area. Blight should always be anticipated and a spray of Zineb or copper given in mid-July. Early July is not too early in the more humid districts. This should be followed by further spraying at 10- to 14-day intervals. If the foliage becomes badly attacked it should be cut off and all the leaves removed from the rows and all

tubers carefully examined for signs of disease when in store. It is essential that potato crops are rotated because several troubles can affect them if they are grown on the same ground more than one season in four or five.

Tomatoes. This crop when grown outdoors can be seriously affected by potato blight. It shows clearly as a black diseased area at the stalk end of the fruit. Spraying as for potatoes will minimize the trouble.

Turnips. This crop is often very seriously damaged in the young stages by flea beetle. It can also be attacked by club root. For controls see the paragraph on Brassicas and also page 52.

These are the more common pests and diseases likely to be met with in your garden. There are many more but by good cultivation and a study of the plants needs neither pests or disease should bother the grower unduly. A close watch on the crops will soon reveal any likely trouble and immediate steps should be taken to remedy matters.

It is seldom that just one spraying or dusting will completely eradicate the threat and a further application will usually be needed. When spraying or dusting be sure to direct the spray or dust on the undersides of the leaves as well as on the surface. This is particularly necessary in the case of red spider, potato or tomato blight. In the latter case new growth will be unprotected hence the need for regular spraying.

19 *Vegetables for freezing*

Throughout this book stress has been laid on the value of fresh vegetables picked or dug in prime condition and used immediately. But there are occasions even in the best run gardens when more produce is available than can be used at once. Crops such as peas and beans rapidly pass their prime and so we can either look for an outlet among friends or attempt to preserve the surplus for future use. Some years ago home preservation was by bottling or canning but these methods tend to be laborious and the nature of the process may destroy much of the flavour and food value. Nowadays the housewife can preserve many surplus vegetables by deep freezing them while still in prime condition. Any surplus vegetables can then be kept for use in days of scarcity or when the crop is out of season. Indeed, where space permits many of my gardening friends now plan their vegetable production with deep freezing in mind. Larger sowings are made than would normally be required for day-to-day use and in this way a good store of frozen vegetables can be built up.

The larger type of freezer is the most economical to buy for it can be used to store not only vegetables but fruit, meat and fish. For the average family a freezer of 12 to 15 cubic feet capacity would seem to be a useful size. The chest type, that is one with a top lid, is excellent as there is very little air movement when the lid is lifted. Remember, however, that it is not too easy to reach into the bottom and if you are not one of the athletic types an upright or front-opening model may be more convenient.

If space in the kitchen is limited a freezer can be installed in the garage, basement or shed provided it is dry and an electrical point is handy. It is a good plan to have no other electrical apparatus on the same socket as I know from experience how easy it is to switch off the supply to the freezer. Actual processing methods have not been dealt with here and are best left to specialist publications. It is suggested, however, that individual packs are of a size related to family requirements as by this method the waste of thawed vegetables can be avoided.

Here are a few suggestions as to suitable vegetables and varieties for freezing. Asparagus forms a most useful crop for freezing as it has a relatively short season and is among the more expensive vegetables to buy. The variety Connover's Colossal, the one usually grown, is quite suitable. Broad beans are excellent frozen if gathered while still young. The normal varieties of either spring or autumn sowing are quite suitable.

With regard to dwarf French beans the variety Glamis is particularly recommended for freezing. It is stringless and an excellent cropper. The prince, and Granda are also suitable. Most varieties of runner beans appear to freeze well provided they are gathered young. They are best gathered first thing in the morning. Enorma and Scarlet Emperor are specially recommended for freezing. Small young beetroot of the Early Bunch type make a welcome addition to the stock of frozen vegetables. Brussels sprouts are welcome throughout the year but small, firm buttons must be used and varieties have been developed which give this type of sprout and generally the whole stalk will be ready at one time without an extended cropping period. An example is the F_1 hybrid Thor. The non-hybrid variety Sanda is another good variety to freeze and crops over an extended period. Other older varieties are satisfactory but the sprouts must be firm and small.

Peas for freezing must be very young and you will find the varieties Early Onward, Kelvedon Wonder and Onward very suitable. If you like sweet, small peas try Petit Pois. Young carrots of finger size have a flavour all their own and if frozen at this stage they will be found to be more satisfactory than clamped carrots. Early varieties such as Amsterdam Forcing or Early Nantes are ideal for freezing.

Rhubarb, if frozen early in the season before skinning is necessary, is one of the few things which does not require preliminary preparation. Varieties of summer spinach freeze well either as leaves or as a puree. Sweet corn is another good subject for the freezer. Cut the cobs early in the morning before the sun warms them up. The early varieties should be chosen such as the John Innes Hybrid or Golden Bantam, but do not forget to thoroughly thaw them before cooking or the corn will be cooked while the cob is still frozen. Tomatoes frozen whole become soft on thawing due to the skins being stretched by the expansion of the contents and are better frozen as puree. Choose sun-ripened fruits; your cloches will come in handy here. Most varieties seem satisfactory. Herbs can be frozen when conditions are unsuitable for drying.

The above are some kinds and varieties of vegetables suitable for freezing but the adventurous housewife will want to experiment with other and perhaps more exotic products of the vegetable garden.

Index